Editor

Mary S. Jones, M.A.

Editor in Chief

Karen J. Goldfluss, M.S. Ed.

Cover Artist

Tony Carrillo

Brenda DiAntonis

Imaging

James Edward Grace

Craig Gunnell

Publisher

Mary D. Smith, M.S. Ed.

TCR 5034

DAILY W

Nonfiction Reading

Grade 4

CORRELATED TO COMMON CORE STANDARDS

Includes:

➤ 150 leveled passages with a variety of interesting topics

➤ Comprehension questions that target reading skills & strategies

➤ Standards & Benchmarks

Ideal for test preparation

30 passages & activities in each of these sections:

Interesting Places & Events
Scientifically Speaking
From the Past
Did You Know?
Fascinating People

Teacher Created Resources

Author

Debra J. Housel, M.S. Ed.

CORRELATED TO **COMMON CORE** STANDARDS

Correlations to the Common Core State Standards can be found at *http://www.teachercreated.com/standards/*.

Teacher Created Resources

6421 Industry Way
Westminster, CA 92683
www.teachercreated.com

ISBN: 978-1-4206-5034-1

©2011 Teacher Created Resources

Reprinted, 2013

Made in U.S.A.

Teacher Created Resources

Table of Contents

Table of Contents (cont.)

Introduction

The primary goal of any reading task is comprehension. *Daily Warm-Ups: Nonfiction Reading* uses high-interest, grade-level appropriate nonfiction passages followed by assessment practice to help develop confident readers who can demonstrate their skills on standardized tests. Each passage is a high-interest nonfiction text that fits one of the five topic areas: Interesting Places and Events, Scientifically Speaking, From the Past, Did You Know?, and Fascinating People. Each of these five topic areas has 30 passages, for a total of 150 passages. Each passage, as well as its corresponding multiple-choice assessment questions, is provided on one page.

Comprehension Questions

The questions in *Daily Warm-Ups: Nonfiction Reading* assess all levels of comprehension, from basic recall to critical thinking. The questions are based on fundamental reading skills found in scope-and-sequence charts across the nation:

- recall information
- use prior knowledge
- visualize
- recognize the main idea
- identify supporting details
- understand cause and effect

- sequence in chronological order
- identify synonyms and antonyms
- know grade-level vocabulary
- use context clues to understand new words
- make inferences
- draw conclusions

Readability

The texts have a 4.0–5.0 grade level based on the Flesch-Kincaid Readability Formula. This formula, built into Microsoft Word®, determines readability by calculating the number of words, syllables, and sentences. Multisyllabic words tend to skew the grade level, making it appear higher than it actually is. Refer to the Leveling Chart on page 175 for the approximate grade level of each passage.

In some cases, there are words necessary to a passage that increase its grade level. In those cases, the passage's grade level is followed by an asterisk in the chart. This means that in determining the grade level, the difficult words were factored in, resulting in the increased level shown before the asterisk. Upon the removal of these words, the passage received a grade level within the appropriate range. For example, in the passage, "Australia," the grade level is 5.2. This is because the word *Australia* is repeated several times. Once the word is removed, the grade level is within range.

Including Standards and Benchmarks

The passages and comprehension questions throughout this book correlate with McREL (Mid-Continent Research for Education and Learning) Standards. Known as a "Compendium of Standards and Benchmarks," this resource is well researched. It includes standards and benchmarks that represent a consolidation of national and state standards in several content areas for grades K–12. (See page 6 for the specific McREL Standards and Benchmarks that correspond with this book.) These standards have been aligned to the Common Core State Standards. To view them, please visit *http://www.teachercreated.com/standards/*.

Introduction (cont.)

Practice First to Build Familiarity

Initial group practice is essential. Read aloud the first passage in each of the five topic areas and do its related questions with the whole class. Depending upon the needs of your class, you may choose to do the first three passages in each topic area as a whole class. Some teachers like to use five days in a row to model the reading and question-answering process at the start of the year. Model pre-reading the questions, reading the text, highlighting information that refers to the comprehension questions, and eliminating answers that are obviously incorrect. You may also want to model referring back to the text to ensure the answers selected are the best ones.

Student Practice Ideas

With *Daily Warm-Ups: Nonfiction Reading* you can choose to do whole-class or independent practice. For example, you can use the passages and questions for the following:

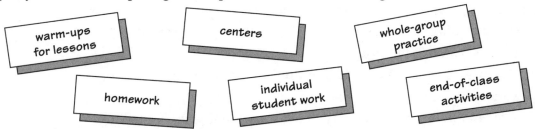

warm-ups for lessons

centers

whole-group practice

homework

individual student work

end-of-class activities

Whichever method you choose for using the book, it's a good idea to practice as a class how to read a passage and respond to the comprehension questions. In this way, you can demonstrate your own thought processes by "thinking aloud" to figure out an answer. Essentially this means that you tell your students your thoughts as they come to you.

Self-Monitoring Reading Strategies

Use the reading strategies on page 174 with your students so they can monitor their own reading comprehension. Copy and distribute this page to your students, or turn it into a class poster. Have your students use these steps for this text, as well as future texts.

Record Keeping

In the sun image at the bottom, right-hand corner of each warm-up page, there is a place for you (or for students) to write the number of questions answered correctly. This will give consistency to scored pages. Use the tracking sheet on page 176 to record which warm-up exercises you have given to your students. Or distribute copies of the sheet for students to keep their own records.

How to Make the Most of This Book

- ✐ Read each lesson ahead of time before you use it with the class so that you are familiar with it. This will make it easier to answer students' questions.

- ✐ Set aside 10 to 12 minutes at a specific time daily to incorporate *Daily Warm-Ups: Nonfiction Reading* into your routine.

- ✐ Make sure the time you spend working on the materials is positive and constructive. This should be a time of practicing for success and recognizing it as it is achieved.

The passages and comprehension questions in *Daily Warm-Ups: Nonfiction Reading* are time-efficient, allowing your students to practice these skills often. The more your students practice reading and responding to content-area comprehension questions, the more confident and competent they will become.

Standards and Benchmarks

Each passage in *Daily Warm-Ups: Nonfiction Reading* meets at least one of the following standards and benchmarks, which are used with permission from McREL. Copyright 2011 McREL. Mid-continent Research for Education and Learning. 4601 DTC Boulevard, Suite 500, Denver, CO 80237. Telephone: 303-337-0990. Web site: *www.mcrel.org/standards-benchmarks*. Correlations to the Common Core State Standards can be found at *http://www.teachercreated.com/standards/*.

Uses the general skills and strategies of the reading process

- Establishes a purpose for reading
- Makes, confirms, and revises simple predictions about what will be found in a text
- Uses phonetic and structural analysis techniques, syntactic structure, and semantic context to decode unknown words
- Uses a variety of context clues to decode unknown words
- Understands level-appropriate reading vocabulary
- Monitors own reading strategies and makes modifications as needed
- Understands the author's purpose

Uses skills and strategies to read a variety of literary texts

- Reads a variety of literary passages and texts

Uses skills and strategies to read a variety of informational texts

- Reads a variety of informational texts
- Uses text organizers to determine the main ideas and to locate information in a text
- Summarizes and paraphrases information in texts
- Uses prior knowledge and experience to understand and respond to new information
- Understands structural patterns or organization in informational texts

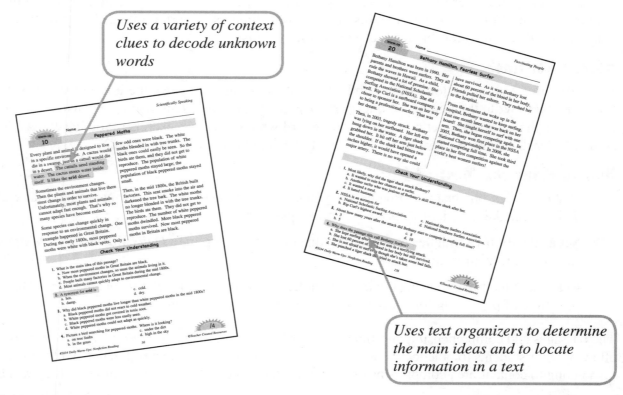

Uses a variety of context clues to decode unknown words

Uses text organizers to determine the main ideas and to locate information in a text

Interesting Places and Events

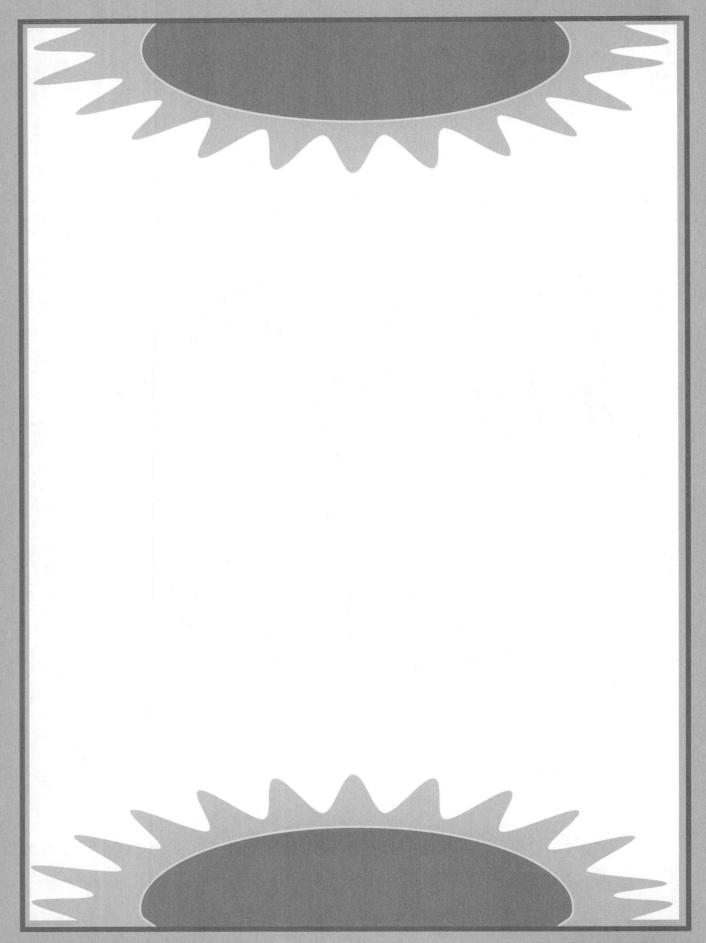

Warm-Up 1

Name _____

Australia

Australia is the only nation that is also a continent. It is the smallest and flattest continent, too. Aborigines have been living there for about 60,000 years. Now whites make up most of the population. They started to arrive in 1788. First, Great Britain claimed Australia as a group of six colonies. Then, it sent its prisoners there to live! Most had committed small crimes. Others had just been unable to pay their bills.

In 1851, gold was found in Australia. As a result, the population more than doubled in ten years. Gold seekers rushed there. But there wasn't much gold. Most men didn't find enough to buy a ticket home on a ship. They stayed and built homes.

In 1890, Britain gave the colonies their freedom. The colonies decided they each wanted to be a state. They wanted to become one nation. In 1901, the six states joined. They formed the Commonwealth of Australia.

Australia has a dry, sunny climate and lots of large, open spaces. Most people live along the southeastern coast. Many work on cattle and sheep ranches or in mines. (Sheep outnumber the people.) The Aussies fondly call their nation, "The Land Down Under." Why? The whole continent lies below the equator.

Check Your Understanding

1. How many states make up the nation of Australia?
   a. 3
   b. 6
   c. 18
   d. 50

2. What nation sent people to Australia as punishment?
   a. Canada
   b. China
   c. Ireland
   d. Great Britain

3. For about how many years have aborigines been living in Australia?
   a. 60,000
   b. 70,000
   c. 80,000
   d. 100,000

4. Why do you think most of the citizens live along the coast in southeast Australia?
   a. The climate there is always cold.
   b. There are abundant gold mines.
   c. There are important seaports.
   d. There are sheep living in the wild.

/4

Name _____

Warm-Up 2   Hostage Rescue in Peru

In December 1996, people were at a party. It was at the home of the Japanese ambassador in Peru. Three hundred police officers guarded the party. In spite of the extra protection, a group of terrorists attacked. They blew up part of the wall around the house. Then they ran inside. They held the people hostage. This meant that the guests could not leave. The mother of the president of Peru was one of the hostages. The terrorists had guns and bombs. They said they would use them.

At first, both Peru and Japan would not accept the terrorists' demands. But after two months, the president of Japan got scared. He wanted to give in. Instead, the president of Peru took action. First, he sent supplies to the hostages. The hostages got new clothes. They were light colored. This would help rescuers tell them apart from the terrorists. Hidden in the supplies were microphones. They let the police listen in. They found out that the terrorists played soccer at the same time each day in a big room inside the house.

Peruvian soldiers started to dig a secret tunnel under the house. One day the terrorists were playing soccer. The troops blew up just the room where they were. All the terrorists died. Other troops landed on the roof in helicopters. They freed the hostages.

Check Your Understanding

1. The police learned about the terrorists' activities
   a. by watching them through telescopes.
   b. by reading lips.
   c. with cell phone calls.
   d. through hidden microphones.

2. What sport did the terrorists play?
   a. ping-pong
   b. rugby
   c. soccer
   d. badminton

3. How many police were hired to guard the party?
   a. 100
   b. 300
   c. 500
   d. 700

4. Why was this hostage rescue successful?
   a. The rescuers carefully planned and timed their attack.
   b. The terrorists had poor weapons.
   c. The hostages were uncooperative.
   d. The terrorists were not prepared to injure anyone.

/4

Name _____

Big Blast in Siberia

On June 30, 1908, the biggest explosion ever recorded on Earth occurred. It happened in Siberia. Few people live in this part of Russia. No one knows just what happened. Everyone agrees that it's a good thing it happened where it did. Anywhere else on Earth, the loss of life would have been tremendous.

The blast knocked down people and large farm animals more than 400 miles away. It ruined everything within a 24-mile radius. The land was left burned and black. Nothing remained standing. For 20 miles around the center, big trees lay flattened on the ground. They looked like spokes on a bike wheel.

People said they saw something fall from the sky. Then, a blast caused such brightness that it made the sun look dark! During the two months after the blast, sunsets of green and bright yellow occurred all over Europe. The nights never got dark. People could read outdoors at midnight.

Scientists say it was an atomic explosion. But it occurred 36 years before the first atom bomb was created. Small crystals found at the site are like those found in comets. Maybe a comet hit Earth's atmosphere. This would have caused a natural atomic blast. We will probably never know for sure.

Check Your Understanding

1. The big blast in Siberia in 1908 was probably caused by a(n)
   a. atomic bomb.
   b. comet.
   c. earthquake.
   d. UFO crashing.

2. The big blast occurred in a
   a. city.
   b. suburb.
   c. coastal area.
   d. place where few people lived.

3. The Siberian explosion caused changes that people could see in
   a. the sky.
   b. the oceans.
   c. the Himalayan mountains.
   d. nearby volcanoes.

4. If this event had happened someplace other than Siberia,
   a. it would have drained the oceans.
   b. a new valley would have formed.
   c. many people and animals would have died.
   d. there would be no life left on Earth.

/4

Name _____

Warm-Up 4
The Discovery of New Zealand

The first European to discover New Zealand was a Dutch sea captain. His name was Abel Tasman. He worked for the Dutch East India Company. Dutch explorers had already found Australia. They named it New Holland. But they didn't know it was an island. They thought it was a huge continent. They believed that it stretched all the way down to where Antarctica lies.

While searching for this giant continent in 1642, Tasman found the island of Tasmania. (That was not its name at the time. This island was later named after him.) Sailing east from there, Tasman came to a land mass. Natives lived there. They were the Maori. The Maori rowed out to his ship. They attacked and killed four of his crew. Tasman left. He did not try to explore the land.

During the same trip, Tasman sighted New Zealand. He called it Staten Landt. He believed that this land extended across the Southern Ocean all the way to the South American continent.

The next year another Dutch sea captain figured out that it was just a big island. He renamed it Zeelandt. That is Dutch for "sea land." The Maori did not want visitors there, either. So the Dutch didn't follow up on Tasman's discovery. The British captain James Cook finally went ashore there in 1769. He claimed the land for Great Britain.

Check Your Understanding

1. What native tribe lived in New Zealand before Europeans discovered it?
   a. the Hollanders
   b. the Tasmans
   c. the Maori
   d. the Dutch

2. Who went ashore in New Zealand in 1769?
   a. Abel Tasman
   b. James Cook
   c. John James
   d. Abel Cook

3. What does Zeelandt mean in the Dutch language?
   a. big island
   b. eastern land
   c. mysterious island
   d. sea land

4. Why did Great Britain claim land found by the Dutch?
   a. The Dutch gave Great Britain the land as a gift.
   b. The Dutch lost the land after a war with Great Britain.
   c. The Dutch did not want to fight with the natives.
   d. The Dutch sold the land to Great Britain.

/4

Warm-Up

Name _____

5   Maine, the Blueberry State

Maine is the northernmost New England state. It shares a border with Canada. It is the only state that borders just one other state, New Hampshire. It is also the only state to have a one-syllable name.

Maine is the most sparsely populated state east of the Mississippi River. This means it has the fewest people per square mile. That may be because pine forests cover 90 percent of its land. Maine has 3,500 miles of rocky coast. More than 60 lighthouses dot its shores. The seawater never warms up enough to swim in. Many lakes there never get warm enough for swimming, either.

If you dislike storms, move to Maine. It has fewer thunderstorms than any other state east of the Rockies. It has less than 20 per year. Few hurricanes batter this state. By the time they get that far north, they are just rain. However, Maine has its share of winter snow.

Maine makes lumber and paper products. It has the world's biggest toothpick factory. It makes 20 million per day! This state produces a lot of food, such as lobsters, fish, chickens, eggs, and dairy products. Although it's not Maine's nickname, it is the blueberry state. It grows 25 percent of all North America's blueberries. Nowhere else on Earth grows as many.

Check Your Understanding

1. Maine does not have many
   a. lighthouses.
   b. thunderstorms.
   c. miles of sea coast.
   d. pine forests.

2. What nation shares a border with Maine?
   a. Canada
   b. New Hampshire
   c. Mexico
   d. New England

3. How many toothpicks are made daily in Maine?
   a. 2,000
   b. 20,000
   c. 200,000
   d. 20,000,000

4. Why does Maine have so many lighthouses?
   a. The state has lots of stone with which to build lighthouses.
   b. The state has a long, rocky seacoast.
   c. The state is thickly forested.
   d. The state has the world's busiest seaports.

/4

Warm-Up 6

Name _____

The Death of the Aral Sea

Water covers more than 70 percent of Earth's surface. But just three percent is fresh water. And two percent of that fresh water is polar ice. That leaves just one percent for everyone on Earth to use.

The Aral Sea is in central Asia. It is in the nation of Uzbekistan. The Aral Sea was once Earth's fourth-largest lake. But it has been shrinking since the 1960s. Rivers had fed the sea. Then, the rivers' courses were changed to send water to cotton crops in another nation. By 2007, the Aral Sea had lost 90 percent of its water. It shrank into three tiny lakes. Now ships lie stranded in sand that was once the seabed.

The sea had a fishing industry. That is gone. The people there are poor. The sea was so large that it affected the local weather. Now the summers are hotter and drier. The winters are colder and longer. The sea's evaporation left layers of highly salted sand. In March 2010, a sandstorm made many people get sick from breathing the sand.

A nearby nation, Kazakhstan, wants to rebuild the North Aral Sea. It built a dam in 2005. Three years later the water level had risen by 39 feet. But even if this lake can be saved, it will never be the size it once was.

Check Your Understanding

1. By 2007, the Aral Sea had lost how much of its water?
   a. 3 percent
   b. 70 percent
   c. 90 percent
   d. 95 percent

2. The Aral Sea was once the
   a. largest lake in the world.
   b. second-largest lake in the world.
   c. third-largest lake in the world.
   d. fourth-largest lake in the world.

3. How much of Earth's fresh water is trapped in polar ice?
   a. none
   b. 1 percent
   c. 2 percent
   d. 3 percent

4. Why won't the Aral Sea ever return to its original size?
   a. All the rivers' water would have to be redirected.
   b. Global warming will keep the lake from refilling.
   c. Sandstorms will keep the lake from refilling.
   d. It cannot support enough fish.

/4

Name _____

The Year Without a Summer

After years of silence, a volcano awoke in 1815. It stood on an island in Indonesia. Mount Tambora had formed over millions of years. Lava had flowed up from the sea floor until the volcano towered 13,000 feet above the sea. Yet it had stood quietly for a long time.

Mount Tambora erupted on and off for three months. It was the worst volcanic disaster in recorded history. Huge amounts of lava, ash, and deadly gases killed every plant there and on all nearby islands.

It caused trouble for people on the other side of the world, too. In 1816, the northeastern part of the United States and Canada had a "year without a summer." The summer months came but the weather was strange. It never got warm. It snowed in June. Each month had a killing frost. Although farmers planted crops, they died. The frost killed the plants.

At the time, no one knew for sure what was happening. Now we know that the volcano threw dust and ash into the sky. There was so much in the air that it blocked the sunlight. The sun's rays could not get through. This kept North America colder than usual. It took a whole year for most of the ash to fall to the ground. Then temperatures went back to normal.

Check Your Understanding

1. What is the main idea of the passage?
   a. During the summer of 1816, nobody knew what caused the strange weather.
   b. A volcano erupted in 1815, killing many people in the northeastern United States and Canada.
   c. Mount Tambora's eruption caused an odd summer on the other side of the world.
   d. Mount Tambora had formed from a volcano on the sea floor.

2. After the strange summer season, the people living in the northeastern U.S. and Canada faced a grim winter. Why?
   a. They were freezing due to huge blizzards.
   b. There were hungry because their crops had failed.
   c. They lived in the path of an erupting volcano.
   d. They were buried by tons of ash falling from the sky.

3. What did *not* contribute to every plant on the island dying?
   a. deadly gases   c. lack of water
   b. lava   d. ash

4. Could there ever be another year without a summer?
   a. Yes, if another volcanic eruption sent enough ash into the atmosphere.
   b. Yes, but only if multiple volcanoes erupted at the same time.
   c. No, we now have space technology that could prevent ash from blocking the sun.
   d. No, scientists today know how to control volcanoes.

/4

Warm-Up

8

Name _____

The Faces of Mount Rushmore

Each year, many people go to see a cliff in South Dakota. Mount Rushmore has four men's heads carved into its rock. Each head is 60 feet tall! It took workers 14 years to form them. They had to drill, chip, and blast to shape the hard rock into faces. The work was hard. The men wore ropes to keep them safe. The second head started to crumble. They had to blast it away. Then they carved the head in a new spot. The rock that the men chipped away lies in a big pile under the heads.

Who are the four heads? George Washington, Thomas Jefferson, Theodore Roosevelt, and Abraham Lincoln. All of these men were U.S. presidents. Each man did something important for the American people. Mount Rushmore honors them.

George Washington was America's first president. Thomas Jefferson was the third president. He wrote the Declaration of Independence. It told the British king that Americans would rule themselves. Abraham Lincoln ended slavery. Theodore Roosevelt made sure that beautiful parts of the nation became national parks. That way no one could own the land. Everyone could enjoy these places.

Check Your Understanding

1. Where is Mount Rushmore located?
   a. Washington, D.C.
   b. South Dakota
   c. North Dakota
   d. Panama

2. Which event occurred last?
   a. The second head crumbled.
   b. The men worked for 14 years.
   c. People came from all over to see the mountain.
   d. The four men on the mountain were presidents.

3. Why did the second head probably start to crumble?
   a. A bomb hit it.
   b. There was an earthquake.
   c. It was struck by lightning.
   d. There were cracks in the rock that got worse as the men carved it.

4. On Mount Rushmore, the heads are not in the order in which the men served as president. This is probably because the builders
   a. put the faces in order of the presidents' popularity.
   b. put each face where it best matched the natural rock face.
   c. didn't know the order in which the men served as president.
   d. weren't told whose faces they were carving until they were almost done.

/4

Warm-Up

9

Name _____

The Smithsonian Institute

An English scientist named James Smithson died in 1829. He left a lot of money to the United States. This was odd. He had never even visited the nation. His will said the funds must be used to increase knowledge among all people. The U.S. government had to think of a way to do that. It chose to create a research museum. It is the Smithsonian Institute. It is in Washington, D.C.

The first building was called the Castle. But the Institute soon outgrew it. Today it has many buildings. There is a museum of American art, an air and space museum, and a museum of American history. There is a museum of African art, a museum of natural history, and a postal museum. The American Indian museum and the national zoo are part of it, too.

The Smithsonian has one of the largest collections on Earth. It owns more than 137 million items. Some are artwork, some are scientific, and others are historic. It displays just two percent of those items. The rest are available for research. The collection is changed from time to time.

Best of all, it is free to see everything. Each year, more than 25 million people visit. It does just what Smithson had hoped. It increases knowledge.

Check Your Understanding

1. How many items does the Smithsonian Institute own?
   a. more than 137 million   c. more than 371 million
   b. more than 173 million   d. more than 731 million

2. How many times did James Smithson visit the United States?
   a. zero   c. two
   b. one   d. He didn't visit; he lived in the United States.

3. Which of the Smithsonian buildings was built first?
   a. the Museum of African Art   c. the Castle
   b. the Air and Space Museum   d. the American Indian Museum

4. Why would Smithson donate his money to the United States?
   a. England had mistreated him.
   b. America was growing fast and needed an educated public.
   c. He had a careless lawyer who made a mistake in his will.
   d. He wanted a building named after himself.

/4

Warm-Up
10

Name _____

The Rocky Mountains

The Rocky Mountains is the largest mountain chain in North America. It stretches for more than 3,000 miles. The mountains start in western Canada. They go all the way to New Mexico. The Rockies form the Continental Divide. This means that all the rivers to the east of the mountains flow to the Atlantic Ocean. All the rivers to the west flow to the Pacific Ocean.

Crossing the Rockies is not easy. So people built tunnels. Two famous tunnels cut through peaks. At more than 11,000 feet above sea level, Eisenhower Memorial Tunnel is the world's highest highway tunnel. Moffat Tunnel is one of the longest railroad tunnels in the United States.

The Rockies are so tall that they affect the nation's weather. The weather along the West Coast is mild. This is true year-round. The weather on the East Coast is stormy and unsettled. The Rockies cause both these weather patterns. Storms form near the Rockies. They move from west to east. Areas to the east of the Rockies get blasted with cold air, too. It roars down from Canada. On the west side of the Rockies, this hardly ever occurs.

When warm and cold fronts bump into each other east of the Rockies, storms form in the Midwest. Once a storm forms, it can go for thousands of miles. It can blow all the way to the Atlantic Ocean.

Check Your Understanding

1. The world's highest road tunnel is
   a. not named in this article.
   b. Moffat Tunnel.
   c. Continental Divide Tunnel.
   d. Eisenhower Memorial Tunnel.

2. Due to the Rockies, the West Coast weather is
   a. much colder than the East Coast.
   b. about the same as the East Coast.
   c. more stormy than the East Coast.
   d. more calm than the East Coast.

3. What is the approximate length of the Rocky Mountain chain?
   a. 3,000 miles
   b. 6,000 miles
   c. 11,000 miles
   d. 13,000 miles

4. Why were tunnels built through the Rocky Mountains?
   a. Tunnels cost very little to build.
   b. People hoped it would cause better weather.
   c. Some of the peaks are so tall that a road would be too steep.
   d. Tunnels have more beautiful scenery than roads would.

/4

Warm-Up

Name _____

11   Rhode Island, the Smallest State

You may know that Rhode Island is the nation's smallest state. But did you know that it is not an island? This state is part of the U.S. East Coast mainland. Rhode Island has 36 islands. The largest is Aquidneck Island. It was once called Rhode Island. The whole state is named for it.

In 1630, Roger Williams started the Rhode Island colony. He wanted people to have religious freedom. The Puritans in the Massachusetts Bay Colony were rigid. They threw out people whose faith was different. Those people went to Rhode Island.

Richard Arkwright invented a spinning machine. People who worked in his factory were not allowed to leave England!

But Samuel Slater did. He snuck onto a ship. When he reached Rhode Island in 1793, he built the machine from memory. This started the state's cloth-making industry.

Now 90 percent of the people in Rhode Island live in cities. Just 15 percent work in industry. Two-thirds of them work in service jobs. Some fish the waters of the Atlantic for lobsters, tuna, and clams.

In 1981, this state hosted the longest game in baseball history. The Pawtucket Red Sox and the Rochester Red Wings played 32 innings. It took two days. And the game was still tied! The game was resumed two months later. In the 33rd inning, the PawSox won.

Check Your Understanding

1. This island used to be called Rhode Island. What is its name today?
    a. Aquidneck Island   c. Williams Island
    b. Long Island   d. Arkwright Island

2. Who built the first spinning machine in Rhode Island?
    a. Richard Arkwright   c. Roger Williams
    b. Samuel Slater   d. Thomas Rhodes

3. What percent of Rhode Islanders do *not* work in industry?
    a. 15 percent   c. 66 percent
    b. 32 percent   d. 85 percent

4. It was illegal for English spinning workers to leave the nation because the factory owners
    a. were desperate for workers.
    b. paid the best wages.
    c. did not want to reveal how they made cloth.
    d. wanted to keep their workers happy.

/4

Warm-Up

12

Name _____

The Amazon Rain Forest

The Amazon tropical rain forest is huge. It is bigger than all Earth's other tropical rain forests put together. It lies in parts of nine nations in South America. It covers an area two-thirds the size of mainland United States. Its climate has been the same for millions of years. Even the ice ages did not affect it. It is always rainy and warm. The high humidity and average temperature of 86°F varies little from day to night.

The rain forest has four layers. Plants and animals live in each one. The first is the forest floor. There, microbes break down fallen trees and dead animals within days. Poison dart frogs, snakes, jaguars, and alligators live there.

The understory is the second level. It lies between the floor and 60 feet high. It has humidity of 90 percent, no wind, and little sunlight. Slow-moving sloths hang from tree branches there. The third level, called the canopy, has the largest number of plants and animals. Above it, the emergent layer has lots of sun and high winds. Monkeys, colorful parrots, and eagles live there.

The Amazon has more types of plants than all those found in the United States. Half of the world's plant species live there. Some important drugs come from these plants. They fight deadly diseases like cancer and malaria.

Check Your Understanding

1. Which animals live on the forest floor?
   a. sloths
   b. monkeys
   c. jaguars
   d. eagles

2. What is the average temperature in the rain forest?
   a. 60°F
   b. 86°F
   c. 68°F
   d. 90°F

3. The Amazon rain forest is part of how many South American nations?
   a. two
   b. three
   c. six
   d. nine

4. Why do parrots live in the emergent layer?
   a. It would be too hard to fly in the thick, dark lower layers.
   b. The scenery is the prettiest in the emergent layer.
   c. The birds enjoy playing with the monkeys.
   d. They need plentiful sunshine in order to fly.

/4

Warm-Up

13

Name _____

The Galapagos Islands

Ecuador lies on South America's west coast. This nation owns the world's most unusual islands. They lie 600 miles off the coast. The Galapagos Islands are 18 small landmasses. They are right on the equator. Some of Earth's most unique plants and animals live there.

These islands have volcanoes, swamps, and forests. One volcano erupted in 2009. Sea currents cause four different environments. Cold water surrounds the islands. Warm winds blow over the land. So animals that live in cold and warm places **coexist**. Both penguins and iguanas live there.

The Islands' plants and animals are like those of South America. Scientists think that heavy rains made huge chunks of land break off. They were swept down rivers. They floated out to sea. They ran into the islands. The plants and animals on these chunks of land had to adapt or die. The iguanas learned to swim. Why? The only thing to eat was seaweed. Marine iguanas do not live anywhere else.

The Charles Darwin Research Station is on the largest island. Scientists there study the wildlife. Just one island has a source of fresh water. This means few people live there. Ecuador has made the Galapagos Islands into a national park. About 40,000 tourists visit each year.

Check Your Understanding

1. Where did the plants and animals in the Galapagos Islands originally come from?
   - a. South America
   - b. North America
   - c. Central America
   - d. Australia

2. Which event occurred first?
   - a. The iguanas couldn't find enough to eat.
   - b. The pieces of land came to an island group.
   - c. Heavy rain washed pieces of land into the sea.
   - d. The iguanas learned how to swim.

3. What makes Galapagos iguanas different from all other iguanas?
   - a. They do not eat green plants.
   - b. They eat green plants.
   - c. They do not know how to swim.
   - d. They know how to swim.

4. The word **coexist** means
   - a. attack each other.
   - b. live side by side.
   - c. avoid each other.
   - d. ignore each other.

/4

Warm-Up

14   The California Gold Rush

Name _____

Gold is a rare metal. People have wanted it for thousands of years. It does not rust like other metals. Kings and queens wore it as jewelry. Gold coins were one of the first kinds of money. Whenever gold was found, it caused a gold rush. People hurried to the place where the gold was found. They wanted to get rich.

There have been several gold rushes in American history. The biggest one happened in California. A man found gold there in 1848. People living in the East raced across a vast wilderness. They went to the West Coast. Some people came from other nations. Once a person arrived, he had to stake a claim. This meant he had to file papers to own a piece of land. Then any gold on that land belonged to him. Many people looked for gold nuggets in streams. They used a sieve in the moving water. Sometimes the gold could be dug from the ground.

So many gold miners came to California during 1849 that people called them the "forty-niners." San Francisco had been a small town. It quickly became a city of 25,000 people! So many people came to the area that California had enough people to become a state by 1850.

Check Your Understanding

1. In 1849, most of the people heading to California went to
   a. get the area admitted to the Union as a state.
   b. look for oil.
   c. find gold.
   d. get free farmland.

2. Which event occurred second?
   a. Most gold mines dwindled and finally disappeared.
   b. Thousands of men raced to California.
   c. Someone found gold in California.
   d. California had enough people to qualify for statehood.

3. Why do people seek gold?
   a. because they want to be royalty
   b. because they want to be famous
   c. because they want to be healthy
   d. because they want to be wealthy

4. Picture a "forty-niner" miner looking for gold. He is using a
   a. jackhammer.
   b. backhoe.
   c. rake.
   d. shovel.

/4

Warm-Up

15   The Earthquakes of 2010

Name _____

The year 2010 saw two strong quakes. The first occurred on January 12. It hit the Caribbean island nation of Haiti. Its strength was a 7.0 on the Richter scale. (On this scale, 10 is the worst. There has never been a 10 in recorded history.) The quake wrecked the main port. It ruined much of the capital city of Port-au-Prince. More than 220,000 people died. More than a million people lost their homes. A strong aftershock hit the area eight days later. Aftershocks are smaller earthquakes. They happen in the weeks after a big one.

On February 27, another earthquake occurred. This one was off the shore of Chile in South America. It was an 8.8 on the Richter scale. This means it was 500 times stronger than the Haitian quake. About 800 people died. Why did the stronger quake have a lower death toll? The answer is building codes. In a quake, falling buildings kill many people. Chile has strict building codes. Buildings there must be earthquake-proof. This is a wise measure. The nation of Chile has had four of the strongest earthquakes in recorded history. In fact, in 1960, it had a 9.5. That is the most powerful quake ever recorded.

Haiti has no building codes. The nation had not had a strong earthquake in 200 years. The government did not foresee the danger.

Check Your Understanding

1. The Chile quake in February 2010 had a Richter scale strength of
   a. 7.0.
   b. 8.8.
   c. 8.9.
   d. 9.5.

2. When did a strong aftershock strike Haiti?
   a. the passage does not say
   b. January 12, 2010
   c. January 20, 2010
   d. February 27, 2010

3. In what year was the world's most powerful earthquake recorded?
   a. 1960
   b. 1997
   c. 2004
   d. 2010

4. You can conclude that many of the Haitians died when
   a. many fires started after the quake.
   b. falling buildings crushed them or caused bad injuries.
   c. cracks in the ground opened and swallowed them.
   d. dams burst, releasing a wave of water on Port-au-Prince.

/4

Name _____

Warm-Up 16   The Cruelest Month in American Mining

Mining is dangerous. In July 2002, coal miners were working in the Quecreek Coal Mine in Pennsylvania. Suddenly, water gushed into the mineshaft. Nine men ran for the elevator. It would take them to the surface. But the water got there first. The men turned. Breathing in a small space near the ceiling, they ran on a conveyor belt to higher ground.

The mine's owners had to drill a hole to get air to the miners. If the men were still alive, they would go to the highest spot. The owners found the coordinates of the highest shaft. Then they used GPS* to find the right spot in the field. At last, more than three days after the accident, the rescue crew broke into the mineshaft. All the miners survived.

That story had a happy ending, in large part because of today's technology. But there didn't used to be much that anyone could do to help after a disaster. December 1907 was the worst month in mining history. On December 1, the Naomi Mine blast killed 34 people. Five days later, an explosion sealed 361 miners in Monongah Mine. On December 16, 58 people died in Yolande Mine. Three days later, 239 miners died in an explosion in Darr Mine. And on the last day of the month, 11 men died in a blast in Carthage.

*Global Positioning System—a system in which three satellites pinpoint an exact spot on Earth's surface and send the information to a receiver

Check Your Understanding

1. Which disaster had the highest death toll?
   a. Yolande Mine
   b. Darr Mine
   c. Monongah Mine
   d. Carthage Mine

2. How many miners survived for three days after a flood in the Quecreek Coal Mine?
   a. none
   b. 9
   c. 11
   d. 34

3. What caused the deaths of most of the miners in December 1907?
   a. cave-ins
   b. floods
   c. poisonous gases
   d. explosions

4. Why are there explosions in coal mines?
   a. Explosive gases get trapped in the mines during the mining process.
   b. Many miners act careless with dynamite.
   c. Mine owners store explosive supplies too close to open flames.
   d. Mine owners store bombs in old mine shafts as a favor to the military.

/4

Name _____

17   The Deadly Cloud from Lake Nyos

Lake Nyos lies above an old volcano in Africa. It no longer erupts. But gases from it seep into the lake. Carbon dioxide enters the deepest waters. It stays there just as carbon dioxide stays inside an unopened can of soda. Over time, the carbon dioxide mixed with water. This water was a bit heavier than normal water. So it didn't rise. The weight of the water above it held it down, too.

Then, on August 21, 1986, the carbon dioxide water rose to the top of the lake. Carbon dioxide bubbles formed, just like when you open a can of soda and fizz comes out. These bubbles pulled up more carbon dioxide. Soon billions of bubbles rushed to the surface. The gas burst from the lake. So much gas escaped that the water level dropped three feet!

The carbon dioxide acted like fog. It crept over the surrounding land. If there is too much carbon dioxide in the air, people cannot get enough oxygen. The deadly cloud floated over some towns. About 1,700 sleeping people did not wake up. Cows and wildlife died, too.

Probably a small volcanic eruption occurred under the lake. It pushed up the deep water. Now a pump at the bottom of Lake Nyos runs daily. This makes the deep water lose its carbon dioxide slowly.

Check Your Understanding

1. Lake Nyos lies above a(n)
   a. earthquake fault.
   b. natural spring.
   c. old volcano.
   d. carbon dioxide mine.

2. What happened to 1,700 people near Lake Nyos on August 21, 1986?
   a. They were treated for breathing problems.
   b. They died in their sleep.
   c. They saw all of their cows die.
   d. They went swimming in Lake Nyos.

3. Why did the lake's level drop three feet?
   a. A lot of gas escaped from near the bottom of the lake.
   b. The water turned into steam when the volcano erupted.
   c. The water drained away to another place.
   d. The water shot out of the lake like a fountain, spraying all over the land.

4. How did Lake Nyos most likely form?
   a. Two rivers drained into the lake.
   b. An underground spring fed the lake.
   c. A melting glacier fed the lake.
   d. The volcano left a crater that filled with rainwater over a long time.

/4

Warm-Up
18

Name _____

Signs of Global Warming

Most scientists are certain that global warming is real. The signs are all around us. Greenland is a large island. It is off the coast of Canada. An ice sheet covers much of it year-round. Now its ice is melting. In fact, its loss of ice doubled between 1995 and 2005.

In the whole Arctic Ocean, the amount of ice fell by nine percent from 1978 to 2008. In September 2007, the Northwest Passage was ice-free for the first time in history. The Northwest Passage is a sea route in the Arctic Ocean. It lies above Canada. Since it was never free of ice, ships have not used it.

The ice in the Antarctic is melting, too. Melting polar caps have made the global sea level rise four to ten inches in the past 100 years. This has hurt mangrove forests in Bangladesh and Bermuda. Higher sea levels caused saltwater to mix with the fresh water in which these trees grow.

For the last few decades, parts of Canada, Alaska, and Russia have had warmer temperatures. The permafrost has thawed in some places. (Permafrost is soil that should be frozen all the time.) So we know that the world is heating up. The question is, can we stop it? Can we slow it down? Only time will tell.

Check Your Understanding

1. Which is *not* the result of global warming?
- a. Greenland's ice loss
- b. a rising human population
- c. thawing permafrost
- d. an ice-free Northwest Passage

2. Mangrove trees
- a. need fresh water.
- b. are not damaged by global warming.
- c. need saltwater.
- d. need a mixture of fresh water and saltwater.

3. Which place does *not* have any permafrost?
- a. Alaska
- b. Bangladesh
- c. Canada
- d. Russia

4. How long did it take the Arctic Ocean's ice to fall by nine percent?
- a. 5 years
- b. 10 years
- c. 30 years
- d. 100 years

/4

Warm-Up 19

Name _____

Mount Kilimanjaro

Mount Kilimanjaro is the tallest mountain in Africa. It lies in Tanzania on the border of Kenya. The mountain's slopes have good soil where farmers grow coffee, bananas, and cacao. (Cacao is used to make chocolate.) The mountain has glaciers that feed streams. The water flows down the mountain, bringing water to the valley below. Crops grow there, too.

Mount Kilimanjaro is a volcano. It has not erupted for at least 170 years. Melted rocks lie deep inside it, so steam and sulfur escape from cracks near Uhuru Peak. People stay away from these spots. Sulfur smells like rotten eggs!

Kilimanjaro has two peaks. Uhuru Peak stands 19,340 feet high. That's almost four miles tall! It is very cold at that height. Bitter winds blow, and this peak always has ice and snow. The mountain's other peak is Mawensi. It is 16,890 feet high. It does not have ice or snow.

Each year many people climb this mountain. There are five main trails. It takes about five to eight days to reach the top and come back. Climbers stay in huts that have been built along the way.

Global warming is changing Mount Kilimanjaro. Rising temperatures are making the snow melt faster. Experts think that its glaciers will be gone by 2020.

Check Your Understanding

1. Mount Kilimanjaro is
   a. in Asia.
   b. an old volcano.
   c. near the North Pole.
   d. under a glacier.

2. The name of Mount Kilimanjaro's taller peak is
   a. Tanzania.
   b. Mawensi.
   c. Uhuru.
   d. Kenya.

3. What is the height of Mount Kilimanjaro's shorter peak?
   a. 16,890 feet
   b. 17,000 feet
   c. 19,340 feet
   d. 29,028 feet

4. Which statement is true?
   a. Crops grow on Mount Kilimanjaro's slopes.
   b. Glaciers cover both peaks on Mount Kilimanjaro.
   c. Sulfur escapes near Mawensi Peak.
   d. There are eight main trails up the mountain.

/4

Warm-Up
20

Name _____

Antarctica

Antarctica is the size of the United States and Mexico combined, or about twice the size of Australia. Yet no one owns it. No one lives there all the time. About 39,000 tourists visit each year.

In 1841, the British explorer James Clark Ross went there. He led a team in exploring the icy land. They found Mount Erebus. It is an active volcano. They discovered the Transantarctic Mountains, too. This chain divides the large ice sheets that cover the land. The ice sheets are more than two miles thick. Their weight has made Antarctica's land mass sink below the sea's surface. The ice slowly moves about half a mile a year. It flows to the edge of the continent. When it reaches the shore, huge chunks break off. They float away as icebergs.

More than 90 percent of Earth's permanent ice is there. The ice cover causes 90 percent of the sun's rays to reflect off its surface. Little heat gets absorbed. The coldest temperature ever recorded on Earth occurred in Antarctica. At -128°F, it was colder than Mars.

Antarctica is a desert. It gets little rain or snow each year. The continent spends half of the year in darkness. The sun disappears below the horizon in March. It does not reappear until September.

Check Your Understanding

1. Which continent is half the size of Antarctica?
   a. Australia
   b. Europe
   c. Africa
   d. Asia

2. Who made major discoveries in Antarctica?
   a. an American explorer
   b. a British explorer
   c. a Mexican explorer
   d. an Australian explorer

3. The majority of the world's ice is located in
   a. Australia.
   b. the Arctic Circle.
   c. Antarctica.
   d. Asia.

4. Which statement is false?
   a. Most of the sun's rays reflect off Antarctica.
   b. Antarctica has had the coldest temperature ever recorded on Earth.
   c. Antarctica has an active volcano.
   d. Antarctica's land is mostly above sea level.

/4

Warm-Up 21

Name _____

Bermuda

Bermuda is a nation with 138 islands. It is about 650 miles off the coast of North Carolina. Juan de Bermúdez found it in 1503. He discovered it by accident. The Spanish explorer's ship was blown there during a storm. His crew thought it was an awful place. The cahow is a native bird. It made loud screeches. Wild pigs made scary noises at night. Dangerous coral reefs surrounded the islands. There were fierce storms. The sailors called it the Isle of Devils.

In 1609, a British ship wrecked near Bermuda. Survivors of the *Sea Venture* made it to shore. They liked the land. So the British settled in Bermuda in 1612. They used it as a base for their navy. They launched attacks against the Americans.

(This was during the American Revolution and the War of 1812.)

The Gulf Stream is an ocean current. It warms Bermuda, giving it a subtropical climate. Rain is the only source of fresh water. People collect it from their roofs. Gutters guide the water into storage tanks. Finance is the main business. Tourism is second. The nation is famous for its pink sand beaches and clear seawater. More than 500,000 people visit each year.

Citizens can have just one car. The speed limit is 20 miles per hour. Most people use motor scooters. No billboards, neon lights, or fast-food restaurants are allowed.

Check Your Understanding

1. Who decided to settle in Bermuda?
   a. a Spanish explorer
   b. the survivors of a shipwreck
   c. colonists blown off course on their way to North Carolina
   d. an American explorer

2. The nation of Bermuda is named after
   a. a native bird.
   b. the Gulf Stream.
   c. the first British governor.
   d. the person who discovered it.

3. Picture yourself standing in Bermuda. What won't you see?
   a. people driving cars
   b. freshwater streams
   c. signs for tourists
   d. pink sand beaches

4. From this passage, you can tell that
   a. people don't want to live in Bermuda due to the lack of fresh water.
   b. America fought Great Britain for ownership of Bermuda.
   c. Bermuda's coral reefs were a danger to ships.
   d. wild pigs still frighten people in Bermuda.

/4

Name _____

Warm-Up 22   Mount Vernon

George Washington lived at Mount Vernon in Virginia. George took great pride in his home. He died there in 1799. He and his wife, Martha, are buried there. But by 1850, his mansion was falling apart. A South Carolina woman named Ann Pamela Cunningham thought this was wrong. She wanted people to visit Mount Vernon. She decided to fix it.

This was no easy task. In 1853, Ann created the first national historic preservation group. She and 12 other women formed the Mount Vernon Ladies Association. They needed $200,000. Then they could buy the house and 200 acres of land. That was a huge sum. But the ladies did not give up. They started the first national fundraising campaign. They put ads in lots of newspapers. The ads asked for **donations**. Money came in about $1 at a time. It took the group six years to raise the cash.

The National Historic Preservation Act was passed in 1966. It formed an agency. It takes care of historic sites in the United States. Yet the Mount Vernon estate does not get any federal funds. The women's group is still in charge. It sells tickets. People who want to tour the house and grounds buy these tickets. The money goes to take care of Mount Vernon.

Check Your Understanding

1. Mount Vernon was in bad shape about how many years after George's death?
   a. 5
   b. 10
   c. 50
   d. 75

2. When did the Mount Vernon Ladies Association have enough cash to buy the property?
   a. 1850
   b. 1853
   c. 1859
   d. 1966

3. A **donation** is a
   a. deed to property.
   b. newspaper ad.
   c. ticket.
   d. gift.

4. Which statement is false?
   a. Mount Vernon was built in Virginia.
   b. The National Historic Preservation Agency is now in charge of Mount Vernon.
   c. Martha Washington is buried at Mount Vernon.
   d. Ann Pamela Cunningham formed the Mount Vernon Ladies Association.

/4

Warm-Up

23

Name _____

Key West, Florida

A key is another name for an island. Key West is the southernmost city in the United States. It's on an island of the same name. It is not far from Mexico. The island lies closer to Cuba than to Miami, Florida. Key West has a mild climate. The average temperatures in the winter are just 14°F lower than the summer temperatures! Key West is the only city in the lower 48 states to have never had a frost. Tourists flock there year round.

Ship carpenters built many of the old homes on the island. They used wooden pegs instead of nails. (That's how they put ships together.) In 1860, Key West was Florida's largest and richest city. Those who lived there had the highest income per person in the United States! Why? They **salvaged** goods from shipwrecks. The beautiful chandeliers and fine furniture in the homes amazed visitors. These items came from wrecks. Nearby coral reefs caused many ships to go down.

In the past, the only way to get to Key West was by boat. Then, a railroad was built. Long bridges stretched over the water between islands. A hurricane wrecked the railroad in 1935. It was not rebuilt. Now the Overseas Highway joins the Florida Keys to the mainland. It is 127.5 miles long. It first opened in 1938. It was rebuilt in the 1980s.

Check Your Understanding

1. Key West is
   a. a part of Mexico.
   b. frequently struck by hurricanes.
   c. a part of Cuba.
   d. in the same state as Miami.

2. The word **salvaged** means
   a. ordered.
   b. saved.
   c. organized.
   d. created.

3. Key West
   a. has major temperature changes based on the season.
   b. has a railroad that joins it to the mainland.
   c. never has snow.
   d. is rarely sunny.

4. You can tell that wooden ships were held together by
   a. wooden pegs.
   b. iron nails.
   c. woven bamboo mats.
   d. tropical vines.

/4

Name _____

Warm-Up 24   Without Warning

Pompeii was a busy city in Ancient Rome. It was located near what is now Naples, Italy. The city lay at the base of Mount Vesuvius. It is the only active volcano on Europe's mainland. Back then, the people did not know that it was a volcano.

Before a volcano erupts, it usually rumbles and smokes. But when Mount Vesuvius erupted in 79 CE, it gave no warning. First, the mountain sent out a spray of red-hot rocks and pebbles. They rained down on the city. Next, it put out a dense cloud of toxic gases. This killed all living things. Then, it spewed ash for a week. Tons of it fell on the city. It covered it like a thick blanket. This formed an airtight cover 12 feet deep. It lay undisturbed for over 1,500 years. Since oxygen could not reach the area, things did not rot.

Of the 20,000 people living in Pompeii, about 5,000 escaped. At the first sign of the eruption, the survivors did not grab any belongings. They ran to the Mediterranean Sea. They got into boats and fled. Those who waited even a little while were too late. When they reached the shore, they found that the volcano had caused wild waves. The water swept away both the docks and the boats. This left them stranded.

Check Your Understanding

1. In 79 CE, the people of Pompeii
   a. knew that they were living at the base of an active volcano.
   b. had plenty of time to escape after Mount Vesuvius erupted.
   c. were shocked when Mount Vesuvius erupted.
   d. heard rumbling and saw smoke come from the mountain for weeks before it erupted.

2. Most people died from the
   a. hot rocks and pebbles falling from the sky.
   b. toxic gases.
   c. boiling lava.
   d. thick blanket of ash.

3. What fraction of Pompeii's population survived in this disaster?
   a. one-tenth
   b. one-fourth
   c. one-third
   d. one-half

4. More people didn't escape in boats because the volcano
   a. killed everyone before they could reach the shore.
   b. sunk the boats under a load of red hot rocks and pebbles.
   c. made the boats blow up.
   d. caused waves that wrecked the boats.

/4

Warm-Up

Name _____

25   The Great Yellowstone Fire of 1988

Fire is part of a natural cycle in a forest. Without fire, too many nutrients are tied up in trees. Fire keeps the trees from taking over nearby fields, too. Scientists realized these benefits in 1972. A new national park policy went into effect. It stated that fires caused by lightning strikes would not be fought. Most fires caused by lightning would go out within hours.

However, a fire in Yellowstone National Park in 1988 made rangers drop the policy. It was the driest summer in over 100 years. No rain fell in July. Dead trees lay on the forest floor like logs in a fireplace. On June 14, lightning started a fire. But it didn't go out. After a month, things looked grim. Eight thousand acres had already burned.

On July 21, rangers decided to fight. Two days later, they realized that the fire was beyond control.

Planes and helicopters dumped water on the flames. Firefighters made firebreaks. This means they burned areas in front of the fire. They wanted to take away its fuel. But winds carried bits of burning material across these firebreaks. Winds caused eight separate fires. More than 9,500 firefighters could not stop the fire.

What finally ended it? Snow fell in September. Some areas still smoldered until November. Nearly half the park had burned.

Check Your Understanding

1. How is a forest fire beneficial?
    a. It gives firefighters jobs.
    b. It releases trapped nutrients from plants and trees.
    c. It gives scientists a chance to study forest fires.
    d. It attracts lightning strikes away from people's homes.

2. What happened second during the summer of 1988?
    a. People did not respond immediately.
    b. Lightning caused a forest fire in Yellowstone National Park.
    c. The fire was stopped by snowfall.
    d. New habitats formed.

3. In 1988, a lack of rain caused Yellowstone National Park to
    a. be cooler than normal.   c. have very dry conditions.
    b. support greater plant and animal variety.   d. attract more lightning strikes than usual.

4. Picture Yellowstone in October 1988. What do you see?
    a. Firefighters are spraying water on a huge forest fire.
    b. Most of the trees have colored leaves, and colored leaves blanket the ground.
    c. Tiny pine trees and flowering fireweed are everywhere you look.
    d. There's snow on the ground, and the few standing trees are black and bare.

/4

Warm-Up 26

Name _____

The Bahamas

Did you know that Columbus never set foot on the North American mainland? He landed in what is now the Bahamas. At that time, the Arawak Native Americans lived there. The Spanish did not set up a colony. But they sold the native people as slaves. This left the islands deserted.

In 1650, the British set up a colony there. They used the islands as a base. They went after pirate ships. The pirates kept goods from reaching Great Britain. In 1781, the British lost the American Revolution. American colonists who had sided with them moved to the Bahamas. They set up plantations. They brought African slaves to work on these huge farms. Today, 85 percent of the people living there descended from these slaves.

The Bahamas has 700 islands. They lie south of Florida's tip. The capital city is Nassau. The nation's temperatures are mild. Winter highs are in the 70s. Summer highs are in the 80s. Each year, there are just 25 days when the sun doesn't shine. Astronauts looking down from space say that the Bahamas have the clearest water in the Caribbean. Add to that its white sand beaches, and you have paradise. That's why more than half the citizens work in tourism. Four million people visit each year. Many come on cruise ships.

Check Your Understanding

1. The people who first lived in the Bahamas were the
   a. Spanish.
   b. British.
   c. American colonists.
   d. Arawak.

2. Most of the current Bahamian citizens are the descendants of the
   a. American colonists who sided with the British.
   b. African slaves.
   c. Spanish.
   d. Native Americans.

3. Why do so many Bahamians work in the tourism industry?
   a. There are many visitors needing food, lodging, and services.
   b. There are still large plantations that need to be worked.
   c. It pays well to build cruise ships.
   d. There are no other jobs to do.

4. In the Bahamas, about how many days of the year does the sun shine?
   a. 25
   b. 180
   c. 340
   d. 360

/4

Warm-Up
27

Name _____

Egypt: One Nation, Two Continents

Egypt lies in the northeast corner of Africa. Most of it is in Africa. But its Sinai Peninsula is in Asia. The Suez Canal runs between these two continents. It joins the Mediterranean Sea and the Red Sea. The French built the Canal in 1869. It shortened the distance between Europe and India by 6,000 miles.

Egypt has the second-biggest population in Africa. Its capital is Cairo, the biggest city in Africa. More than nine million people live there. Most Egyptians call themselves Arabs. They speak Arabic. Many people speak English, too. But just half of the adults can read and write.

About 96 percent of the land is desert. Yet one of the world's first societies began here. Why? The Nile River runs through Egypt. It is the world's longest river. Rich farmland lies along its banks. Most of the people live along its banks, too.

Across the land stand rounded towers with lots of holes. These birdhouses are made of mud and clay. Pigeons nest in them. Egyptians eat the birds. They use the birds' droppings as fertilizer. That's important in a country where most people work in farming. They grow cotton, oranges, rice, and sugar cane. The Nile provides the water for the crops.

Check Your Understanding

1. Egypt lies on which two continents?
   a. Africa and Asia
   b. Africa and Europe
   c. Asia and Europe
   d. Asia and Australia

2. The largest city in Africa is
   a. Nile.
   b. Egypt.
   c. Sinai.
   d. Cairo.

3. What is the name of the waterway that connects the Red and Mediterranean Seas?
   a. the Nile River
   b. the Sinai Peninsula
   c. the Suez Canal
   d. the African River

4. Which statement is false?
   a. Egypt has the largest city in Africa.
   b. Egypt is too dry to support agriculture.
   c. The French built a canal in Egypt.
   d. Egyptians speak the Arabic language.

/4

Warm-Up
28

Arizona's Natural Wonders

Name _____

Arizona is a state that borders Mexico. It has two of the world's seven natural wonders. One is the Grand Canyon. The Colorado River formed it. It has taken the river 17 million years to carve this gorge. It is one mile deep. The Grand Canyon's walls have wide stripes of colorful rocks. Five million people visit each year.

The other natural wonder is Meteor Crater. It is a huge hole in the ground. It is almost a mile wide. It formed when a meteor hit about 50,000 years ago. The meteor itself blew up on impact. Just the hole was left. This is the best crater of its kind on Earth.

These two features are world famous. Yet they're not the only interesting things to see in Arizona. More than half the state has mountains and plateaus. Its Painted Desert is a brightly colored plateau. It lies along the Little Colorado River. The rocks in this area seem to change color. At dusk, the rocks look blue, purple, and yellow. At dawn, the same rocks look lilac and blood red.

Arizona also has the nation's largest ponderosa pine forest. But even more spectacular is its petrified forest. It formed 225 million years ago. Water seeped into pine logs. The water left behind mineral deposits. It turned these logs into quartz and opal stones.

Check Your Understanding

1. One of the world's seven natural wonders located in Arizona is
   a. a petrified forest.
   b. the Painted Desert.
   c. the Colorado River.
   d. Meteor Crater.

2. The Grand Canyon
   a. was worn away by the Little Colorado River.
   b. has the nation's biggest ponderosa pine forest along its rim.
   c. has walls that are one mile high.
   d. formed during the past 1 million years.

3. Which statement is false?
   a. The Painted Desert rocks look different colors at various times of the day.
   b. Arizona has a 50,000-year-old meteor in nearly perfect condition.
   c. Arizona's petrified forest formed millions of years ago.
   d. More than half of Arizona has mountains and plateaus.

4. The petrified forest logs have changed into
   a. rocks.
   b. meteors.
   c. plateaus.
   d. a gorge.

/4

Warm-Up
29

Name _____

"Houston, We've Had a Problem"

It was April 1970. Jim Lovell was in command of the *Apollo 13* lunar mission. He was 200,000 miles from Earth. The crew was on its way to the moon. Suddenly an explosion caused a drain of oxygen and electrical power. It left Lovell and his two crewmates, Fred Haise and John Swigert, in trouble. They had less than two hours of oxygen. Swigert radioed NASA, "Houston, we've had a problem."

The crew climbed into the lunar module. Getting into the lunar module kept them from suffocating. But this tiny craft was built to keep two men alive for two days. Now three men sat inside it. They were four days away from home.

Some NASA engineers did long math calculations. They figured out when the men should fire their rockets to get home. Others had to find a way to keep the men breathing. They had to make the remaining oxygen last. To do this, a filter had to be made. Luckily, NASA engineers had a detailed list of what was on board. They knew every item they had to work with. A ground team used just the things that the astronauts had. They designed a makeshift filter. Then they radioed instructions to the crew.

The men splashed down in the Pacific Ocean. Bringing the *Apollo 13* crew home safely was NASA's finest hour.

Check Your Understanding

1. The astronauts first knew that they had trouble when
   a. the lunar module blew up.
   b. Houston contacted them and told them that there was a problem.
   c. they started losing oxygen and electricity rapidly.
   d. they began to suffocate.

2. The astronauts safely landed in the ocean in the
   a. main ship.
   b. service module.
   c. command module.
   d. lunar module.

3. How did the makeshift filter help the crew?
   a. It gave them more electrical power.
   b. It let them have enough oxygen to get home.
   c. It kept the spacecraft from overheating.
   d. It gave them something to do so that they wouldn't panic.

4. Which statement is an opinion?
   a. Bringing home the *Apollo 13* crew was NASA's finest hour.
   b. The explosion happened before the crew had visited the moon.
   c. Jim Lovell, Fred Haise, and John Swigert faced deadly danger.
   d. NASA engineers figured out how to make a makeshift filter.

/4

Warm-Up
30

Name _____

John Brown's Raid on Harper's Ferry

John Brown wanted to end slavery. He decided to take over the U.S. Armory Arsenal and Rifle Works. It held 100,000 guns. He planned to give them to slaves. He thought they would rebel and escape from their owners. The federal arsenal was in the town of Harper's Ferry, Virginia. Two rivers meet at this spot.

During the summer of 1859, Brown's men and arms arrived. They came under cover of night. They hid at the Kennedy Farm in Maryland.

October 16, 1859, was a cold, rainy Sunday night. That's when Brown and 21 men took over the U.S. arsenal. The men seized the bridges over the two rivers, as well. Twelve slaves were freed from nearby farms. Brown's men took the slave owners hostage.

The next day people were angry. They fought against Brown. They killed about half of his men. That night, federal troops arrested Brown and four others. They freed the hostages. No slaves escaped. The raid had failed.

Brown was tried. He was found guilty of murder and treason. In December 1859, he was hanged. The government worried that abolitionists would save him. So it had 1,500 troops encircle the gallows. Brown's actions made his name **synonymous** with anti-slavery beliefs.

Check Your Understanding

1. How many men helped John Brown with the raid?
   a. 12
   b. 21
   c. 35
   d. 59

2. The federal arsenal was the place where
   a. slaves were held before being put up for sale.
   b. John Brown worked.
   c. weapons were stored.
   d. ferry boats were housed.

3. The word **synonymous** means to
   a. be against.
   b. express the same idea.
   c. take strong action.
   d. bring about the end.

4. You can tell that
   a. Kennedy Farm is far from Harper's Ferry.
   b. Brown was willing to take strong action to end slavery.
   c. Brown and his men were in hiding for a year.
   d. the owners of Kennedy Farm participated in the planned raid.

/4

Scientifically Speaking

Warm-Up
1

Name _____

Giant Panda Problems

All the world's wild giant pandas live in a small part of Asia. They are endangered. There are few left. Much of their habitat has been ruined. As the human population grew larger, people took over the land where the pandas once lived.

To make matters worse, giant pandas eat just one food. When an animal relies on only one food, it is vulnerable. Ninety-nine percent of the pandas' food is bamboo. Bamboo is a kind of grass. Yet it grows as tall as a tree. Pandas eat every part of the bamboo. Every part, that is, except for the flowers. Once bamboo flowers, it is no longer tasty or nutritious. Pandas will starve before they will eat flowering bamboo.

So what's the problem? All the bamboo in a forest flowers at the same time. One day there may be lots of tasty bamboo. The next day, the plants flower, drop their seeds, and die! Overnight, it goes from feast to famine. Plus, it will take 5 years before the seeds send up sprouts big enough to eat.

The good news is that bamboo does not flower often. It may take 120 years before a forest blooms. Scientists do not know what causes a bamboo forest to flower. To save the giant pandas, China has stopped logging bamboo. China has also set up dozens of nature reserves for the pandas.

Check Your Understanding

1. About how often does bamboo flower?
   a. once a year
   b. every few years
   c. once in a hundred years
   d. after two weeks of heavy rain

2. What part of bamboo does a giant panda eat?
   a. just the stem
   b. just the leaves
   c. the stem and the flowers
   d. everything but the flowers

3. Which kind of plant is related to bamboo?
   a. a rosebush
   b. a pine tree
   c. a cherry tree
   d. grass

4. Why are giant pandas vulnerable to extinction?
   a. They rely on one food source.
   b. People hunt them.
   c. They are poisoned by bamboo flowers.
   d. Their numbers are increasing.

/4

Warm-Up
2   The Great Alaskan Earthquake

Name _____

The strongest earthquake ever to strike North America happened in Alaska on March 27, 1964. It struck in the late afternoon. The quake caused damage to the city of Anchorage. In some places, the soil changed to a liquid form. Although this fluid state lasted just three minutes, during that time, a chunk of downtown slid into the sea!

Huge cracks opened in the ground, too. Some were 12 feet deep and 50 feet wide. Whole buildings collapsed. Concrete slabs broke free of buildings. They crushed the cars and trucks below. Anchorage's downtown area was flattened. No buildings remained undamaged. Outside of town, landslides buried buildings. Big oil tanks blew up. Several schools caved in. Luckily, no one was inside.

The ground shook for five minutes. Huge waves rolled in from the sea. They pounded towns on the coast. One wave swallowed a dock and the 12 men on it. Another wave picked up a fishing boat. It threw it onto a school's roof one-half mile inland.

For days after the major quake, the people felt 100 small tremors a day. It was a good thing that Alaska didn't have a big population. Although 131 people died, the death toll would have been higher in any other state.

Check Your Understanding

1. Which problem was directly caused by the soil in its liquid form?
   a. giant waves forming on the sea
   b. large parts of the city sliding towards the sea
   c. aftershocks in the following days
   d. huge cracks opening in the ground

2. What is the main idea of this passage?
   a. Alaska's earthquake caused a lot of damage.
   b. The strongest earthquake ever recorded in North America was in Alaska.
   c. More people would have died if the earthquake had hit a larger city.
   d. Anchorage's downtown area was flattened.

3. Which did *not* happen during the Alaskan earthquake?
   a. The ground cracked.
   b. Fires started.
   c. Buildings fell down.
   d. New hills formed.

4. Why did so few people get hurt?
   a. The state had been evacuated before the earthquake.
   b. The people had time to prepare for the disaster.
   c. Alaska was not heavily populated.
   d. All of the buildings in Alaska were built for strong earthquakes.

/4

Warm-Up
3

Name _____

P-U! It's a Skunk!

Skunks live in North America, Central America, and parts of South America. During the summer, they live in hollow trees or piles of hay. In places with cold winters, skunks dig burrows and hibernate. They may share their winter sleeping quarters with raccoons or rabbits. While this may sound strange, the body heat of several animals together keeps them all warmer.

When you see the black and white and bushy tail of a skunk, you probably know to stay back. Skunks have a bad reputation. They spray an awful-smelling oil when they need to protect themselves. Yet skunks don't like their own odor.

They spray as a last resort. On a windy day, they choose to run away rather than spray an enemy. They don't want the stinky oil to get onto their own fur.

Skunks try several things before they spray. As an animal moves closer, the skunk arches its back. It raises its tail in the air in order to look big and scary. Next, the skunk hisses, grinds its teeth, and stamps its feet. If none of those **tactics** work, the skunk may do a "handstand." It may even walk on its front paws! The skunk wants the predator to think it's too big to attack. If the animal keeps coming, the frustrated skunk sprays. It can hit a target up to 16 feet away.

Check Your Understanding

1. If you see a wild skunk, you
   a. will definitely get sprayed.
   b. shouldn't try to get close to it.
   c. should back it into a corner.
   d. should run toward it screaming and waving your arms.

2. The main idea of this passage is that skunks
   a. enjoy smelling bad.
   b. are afraid of getting their oil in their fur.
   c. spray only as a last resort.
   d. may share winter dens with raccoons and rabbits.

3. The word **tactics** means
   a. attacks.   c. advantages.
   b. weapons.   d. actions.

4. In what place would you most likely *not* find a skunk?
   a. Australia   c. Central America
   b. Canada   d. South America

/4

Warm-Up
4

Name _____

Insects

Insects are some of the most successful animals on Earth. They can survive harsh conditions. They reproduce in huge quantities. Without insects, few of us would be alive. Why? They are near the start of many food chains. They provide food for other animals. Still, we think of them as pests.

Mammals, amphibians, reptiles, and fish all have internal skeletons made of bones. Insects have an exoskeleton. It is a structure on the outside of the body. It has no bones, yet it gives the body its form. Some insects have wings. Others don't. All insects have antennae and six legs. They also have three body parts: a head, a thorax, and an abdomen. The legs and wings attach to the thorax. The digestive and reproductive systems are within the abdomen.

Flies are some of the most common insects. The housefly has been around for 65 million years! It survived whatever conditions killed the dinosaurs. Houseflies do not bite. So, if you've ever been bitten by a giant fly, it was a female horsefly. She must drink mammal blood in order to lay her eggs.

There are so many termites on Earth that the gas they pass plays a role in global warming. Termites produce more methane than all of our cars, planes, and factories together! They need gut bacteria to digest the wood that they eat.

Check Your Understanding

1. Which female insects must drink mammal blood?
   a. houseflies
   b. termites
   c. moths
   d. horseflies

2. An exoskeleton is most like the
   a. trunk of a tree.
   b. body of a car.
   c. lid of a pot.
   d. supports on a bridge.

3. It would be a bad idea to kill all insects because
   a. they reproduce in large quantities.
   b. houseflies never bite humans.
   c. they are at the beginning of many food chains.
   d. we need the methane that termites produce.

4. Which of these is *not* a fly body part?
   a. a skeleton
   b. antennae
   c. an abdomen
   d. a thorax

/4

Warm-Up

5

Name _____

Fearsome Fossil

How can a fossil be scary? By imagining the animal from which it came. As you read this, try to picture the American lion. Fossils show it was the largest cat ever to live. It was over 8 feet long. It weighed about 625 pounds. It had the biggest brain compared to its body size, too. (This is true for lions of the past and the present.) A big brain means it was smart. It thought about how to stalk its prey.

The American lion looked a lot like modern lions, but it was bigger. Its teeth were larger, too. Today's African lions can grow to 7 feet in length. The largest ones weigh about 550 pounds.

American lion fossils have been found all over the Americas. Some have been dug up in the Yukon in Canada. Others have shown up in Peru. More than 100 fossils have been found in the La Brea Tar Pits in California. Lions stepped into the tar and got stuck. They died there.

The last American lion died about 11,000 years ago. That's when the last ice age ended. This means that they lived at the same time as the early Native Americans known as the Clovis people.

Check Your Understanding

1. Why were big brains helpful to American lions?
   a. They used their large heads to crush their prey.
   b. If they injured part of their brain, they could still function.
   c. It helped them stalk their prey more skillfully.
   d. They could escape from predators.

2. Can you see an American lion at the zoo?
   a. No, they are extinct.
   b. No, they are all in Africa.
   c. Yes, scientists have recreated them from fossils.
   d. Yes, but only at zoos in California.

3. In what country have fossils of American lions *not* been found?
   a. Peru
   b. England
   c. Mexico
   d. The United States

4. About how much more did a big American lion weigh than a big African lion?
   a. 100 pounds
   b. 75 pounds
   c. 225 pounds
   d. 550 pounds

/4

Warm-Up 6

Name _____

Surprises in the Sea

For a long time, scientists believed that the world's biggest shark, the great white, was the only giant shark still in existence. A great white shark can grow up to 15.8 feet long. It can weigh 2,450 pounds. Then, in 1976, several researchers were in a boat off the shore of Hawaii. The team made a shocking discovery. They caught a new, huge shark. No one had ever documented one before. It was 14.5 feet long and weighed 1,650 pounds. The scientists named it *megamouth*. The megamouth shark is rare. Since the megamouth discovery, only about 50 have been seen or caught. Adding to the mystery, each one caught was a male. Then a female washed ashore in Japan. This was in 1994.

In 2007, a local fisherman went to see the staff at a Japanese marine park. He told them that he had caught a strange-looking eel. The people were interested. They brought cameras and filmed the animal. It was not an eel. It was a frilled shark. No one had ever seen a live one before. They were thought to be extinct. It died quickly. We still don't know about any of its habits.

This means that there may still be strange, new species of sea animals that have not yet been discovered.

Check Your Understanding

1. What would be the best reason for naming the new shark *megamouth*?
 a. It was a male shark.
 b. It was over 14 feet long.
 c. It did not have a mouth.
 d. It had a very big mouth.

2. Who caught the first frilled shark?
 a. Hawaiian researchers
 b. Hawaiian pleasure boaters
 c. a Japanese fisherman
 d. the staff at a marine park

3. Scientists thought that the _____ was extinct.
 a. frilled shark
 b. great white shark
 c. megamouth shark
 d. frilled eel

4. How many years after first finding a megamouth shark did scientists first observe a female?
 a. 5 years
 b. 18 years
 c. 20 years
 d. 22 years

/4

Warm-Up 7

Name _____

Robots at Work

Have you ever seen a robot work? The ones in factories often have an arm. It has a tool on the end. The tool may be a screwdriver, a drill, or another tool. Those without tools do lifting or sorting tasks. The word *robot* came from *robota*, a Czech word that means **drudgery**. Why? Most robots stay in one spot all the time. They do the dull jobs that people don't want to do.

Robots cost manufacturers a lot of money. They want flexible robots that can do different jobs by having their programs changed. Let's say that a robot drills a hole in metal. It has a drill at the end of its arm programmed to drill to a set depth. After a few years, the factory does not want the drilling robot. Now it wants a robot that paints. The robot's program is changed and its drill traded for a spray gun. Then it paints instead of drills.

A few robots have artificial intelligence. A human programmed the computer inside the robot to make choices. Sensors on the robot take readings. The program within the robot uses those readings to make decisions. If a robot's job is to pick up something fragile, the sensors keep the robot from holding it too tightly.

Check Your Understanding

1. The majority of robots
   a. stay in one place all the time.
   b. are used in outer space.
   c. have artificial intelligence.
   d. operate in battlefields.

2. The word **drudgery** refers to a(n)
   a. boring job.
   b. low-paid job.
   c. unpaid job.
   d. exciting job.

3. A factory has a robot that uses a drill. The supervisor wants the robot to use a staple gun instead. Which is true?
   a. The robot needs cameras installed.
   b. The robot must be a flexible one that can have its program modified.
   c. The robot must be a very complex and expensive one.
   d. The robot needs remote-control sensors installed.

4. Only an artificial-intelligence robot can
   a. have sensors.
   b. do a repetitive task.
   c. make choices.
   d. operate in places that are dangerous to humans.

/4

Warm-Up
8

Name _____

Wildfires

Humans have always had an uneasy relationship with fire. Fire can be our friend or foe. As a friend, fire offers warmth, light, and heat for cooking. As a foe, an out-of-control fire can cause ruin and death.

Wildfires are bad for humans and wild animals. Each year, such fires ruin millions of acres. They cost billions of dollars in property loss. Such blazes occur often in places that are hot and dry. California, Texas, and Colorado are often hit. In years with little rainfall, dry tinder is everywhere. Nine of out ten wildfires are started by people. It is usually an accident. A dropped cigarette, burning trash, or a child playing with matches can start a big disaster.

In February 2009, Australia had the worst wildfires ever recorded. Four hundred fires killed 173 people and hurt 414 more.

You may have seen Smokey Bear on a sign. He wears a hat. He holds a shovel. His sign states, "Only YOU can prevent wildfires." Perhaps you've seen ads in which Smokey tells you not to burn trash and to put out your campfire. Smokey was a real bear cub. He was rescued from a wildfire. It happened in New Mexico in 1944. He has been the symbol of fire prevention for more than 65 years.

Check Your Understanding

1. Which of the following is something you should *not* do?
   a. Only let adults use matches.
   b. Be careful around fire.
   c. Leave your campfire burning.
   d. Never burn trash.

2. A wildfire is more likely to happen in Texas than in
   a. California.
   b. Colorado.
   c. New Mexico.
   d. Washington, D.C.

3. How did Smokey Bear become the mascot of fire prevention?
   a. Smokey was a bear rescued from a wildfire in 1944.
   b. Smokey was a bear rescued from a wildfire in 2009.
   c. Campers told forest rangers they'd like a bear for a mascot.
   d. Firefighters told forest rangers they'd like a bear for a mascot.

4. Australia faced its worst wildfires in
   a. 1944.
   b. 1965.
   c. 1983.
   d. 2009.

/4

Warm-Up 9

Name _____

Disrupting Ecosystems

People can damage an ecosystem by bringing in a new species. More than 30 years ago, Asian carp were brought to farms in Arkansas. They were supposed to clean algae from ponds. But flooding swept them into the Illinois River. These fish taste bad. No one wants to eat them. Now they are eating the food of the fish that people do eat. People don't want them to spread into the Great Lakes. They have put in underwater electrical gates to keep them from entering Lake Michigan.

A scientist wanted to create a new breed of silkworm. He imported the gypsy moth from Europe in 1860. The moths escaped. They spread across the United States. They ruined trees. Each year, the National Forest Service sprays forests with agents that kill only gypsy moths.

In the early 1980s, the farmers in Indonesia sprayed their crops with a chemical. They wanted to kill the bugs that ate the rice crop. But the chemicals killed the spiders and bees that ate the bugs. To make matters even worse, the bad bugs grew resistant. This means that the chemicals no longer killed them. There were more of them than ever before! In 1986, the government banned insecticides. Bees and spiders were released. They ate the bad bugs. Slowly their numbers fell.

Check Your Understanding

1. People imported Asian carp to Arkansas in order to
   a. eat them.
   b. get rid of native fish.
   c. clean up ponds.
   d. test underwater electrical gates.

2. What bad effect does a gypsy moth have?
   a. It ruins trees.
   b. Its eats other bugs.
   c. It makes a bad odor.
   d. It gives its prey a small electric shock.

3. What did Indonesian farmers do in the 1980s to stop bugs from attacking their crops?
   a. They sprayed chemicals.
   b. They stopped growing rice.
   c. They banned insecticides.
   d. They killed spiders and bees.

4. What often happens when people bring a new species into a habitat?
   a. It makes people pass new laws.
   b. It changes how animals behave.
   c. It improves an existing problem.
   d. It creates a new problem.

/4

Name _____

Peppered Moths

Every plant and animal is designed to live in a specific environment. A cactus would die in a swamp, just as a cattail would die in a desert. The cattails need standing water. The cactus stores water inside itself. It likes the **arid** desert.

Sometimes the environment changes. Then the plants and animals that live there must change in order to survive. Unfortunately, most plants and animals cannot adapt fast enough. That's why so many species have become extinct.

Some species can change quickly in response to an environmental change. One example happened in Great Britain. During the early 1800s, most peppered moths were white with black spots. Only a few odd ones were black. The white moths blended in with tree trunks. The black ones could easily be seen. So the birds ate them, and they did not get to reproduce. The population of white peppered moths stayed large; the population of black peppered moths stayed small.

Then, in the mid 1800s, the British built factories. This sent smoke into the air and darkened the tree bark. The white moths no longer blended in with the tree trunks. The birds ate them. They did not get to reproduce. The number of white peppered moths dwindled. More black peppered moths survived. Now most peppered moths in Britain are black.

Check Your Understanding

1. What is the main idea of this passage?
   a. Now most peppered moths in Great Britain are black.
   b. When the environment changes, so must the animals living in it.
   c. People built many factories in Great Britain during the mid 1800s.
   d. Most animals cannot quickly adapt to environmental change.

2. A synonym for **arid** is
   a. hot.   c. cold.
   b. damp.   d. dry.

3. Why did black peppered moths live longer than white peppered moths in the mid 1800s?
   a. Black peppered moths did not react to cold weather.
   b. White peppered moths got covered in toxic soot.
   c. Black peppered moths were less easily seen.
   d. White peppered moths could not adapt as quickly.

4. Picture a bird searching for peppered moths. Where is it looking?
   a. on tree limbs   c. under the dirt
   b. in the grass   d. high in the sky

/4

Warm-Up

11   Neat Facts About Your Circulatory System

Name _____

Your circulatory system moves blood through your body. Blood carries oxygen to all your cells. It carries waste away from your cells. Waste leaves your body through your lungs, kidneys, and intestines.

Did you know that in one day, the blood in an adult body travels 12,000 miles? That's the distance from New York City to Australia. Every day! Your heart beats 35 million times each year. During the course of your lifetime, your heart will pump one million barrels of blood.

Your system of blood vessels is 60,000 miles long. That's more than twice the distance around the world at the equator. And don't forget that some of these vessels do gravity-defying feats. They're the ones that pump blood up from your legs to your heart. With each squeeze of your leg muscles, valves inside your veins open and blood is pushed up toward the heart. When the muscles relax, the valves snap shut to keep the blood from flowing backward due to gravity.

Have you ever heard of varicose veins? These leg veins have valves that don't work right. When the valve breaks, the blood flows backwards. It collects inside the vein. The vein becomes enlarged. It hurts. You can help prevent varicose veins by always putting your feet up on a stool when you sit down.

Check Your Understanding

1. What keeps your blood from settling in your feet?
   a. Valves close in veins to stop blood from flowing toward the heart.
   b. Valves close in arteries to stop blood from flowing toward the heart.
   c. Valves close in veins to stop blood from flowing away from the heart.
   d. Valves close in arteries to stop blood from flowing away from the heart.

2. Waste does *not* leave the body through the
   a. lungs.
   b. heart.
   c. intestines.
   d. kidneys.

3. How far does the blood travel in an adult body each day?
   a. 1,200 miles
   b. 6,000 miles
   c. 12,000 miles
   d. 60,000 miles

4. How could you prevent getting varicose veins?
   a. by putting up your feet when you sit down
   b. by getting more exercise
   c. by eating more vegetables
   d. by sleeping for at least 8 hours each night

/4

Warm-Up

12

Name _____

Wind Energy

Today there are more than 157,000 wind turbines on Earth. But we don't have these machines perfected. Wind turbines change less than half of the wind hitting their blades into energy. Engineers are working to improve this.

Often, tall windmills with propeller-like blades are grouped together in wind farms. On a wind farm, dozens of wind turbines are spaced well apart so they don't block each other's wind.

Scientists must consider many factors before building a wind farm. Wind speeds vary from place to place. Some sites are worse than others. An open hilltop that is not blocked by trees is best. Many such hilltops are farm fields. Even on big wind farms, the windmills take up less than one percent of the ground. So, the turbines can stand on land that is farmed. The farmer drives a tractor around them. This lets the land be used for two purposes at once. Some wind turbines have been built in the water offshore to catch the ocean breezes.

Although wind energy causes no pollution, turbines cannot provide all of our electricity. Why? Wind does not blow at a constant speed. It does not blow all the time. Yet we need a supply of electric power that we can depend on. Perhaps someday we will be able to store enough energy when the wind blows.

Check Your Understanding

1. One problem with relying on electricity made by wind power is that
   a. wind power is not renewable.
   b. the wind does not blow all the time.
   c. the turbines take up valuable farmland.
   d. wind power causes air pollution.

2. Wind farms are usually built
   a. in big cities.
   b. by farmers.
   c. on hilltops.
   d. in valleys.

3. Wind engineers are working to find a way to
   a. make the wind blow at a certain temperature.
   b. let farmers use the land on which wind turbines stand.
   c. make the wind blow more consistently.
   d. store the energy created by wind turbines.

4. Why do wind turbines convert less than half the wind hitting them into energy?
   a. Engineers have not perfected them yet.
   b. They block each others' wind.
   c. We don't need them to generate very much energy.
   d. There aren't enough wind turbines on Earth.

/4

Warm-Up

13

Killer Bees Calming Down

Name _____

Some South Americans tried to change their honeybees. In 1955, they imported African bees. The people thought these bees would breed with the native bees. Their offspring would be more productive honeybees. The new bees would make more honey. The new bees would pollinate more crops, too. Then there would be a larger harvest of fruits and vegetables. Well, that was the plan. But things didn't work out that way. When the African bees bred with the gentle native ones, the bees became dangerous. These scary bees are known as "killer bees."

Rather than build hives, these bees nest in the ground. When a person comes near, they send out huge swarms of guard bees.

They have five times the number of guard bees than normal honeybees have. The killer bees follow carbon dioxide. That's what we breathe out. They can chase a person for many yards and may cover his or her body with stings. People can die from getting so many stings.

The good news is that some of the killer bees were productive honey makers. Yet they were not too aggressive. So, beekeepers started breeding these calmer bees together. Now these bees have become the norm for beekeeping in Brazil. Beekeepers are getting control over the bees in Mexico, too.

Check Your Understanding

1. Humans bred South American and African bees
   a. by accident; they didn't mean to.
   b. to make more productive honeybees.
   c. to make better guard bees.
   d. because South American bees were too aggressive.

2. Guard bees follow people by
   a. following the carbon dioxide we exhale.
   b. smelling our body odor.
   c. seeing the movement when we run.
   d. hearing us breathe.

3. Why have people died from killer bee attacks?
   a. Just one killer bee's venom can give a person a stroke.
   b. The bees follow the carbon dioxide right into a person's lungs.
   c. Guard bees chase the people until they have heart attacks.
   d. The people receive multiple stings.

4. Bees help farmers by
   a. pollinating fruits and vegetables.
   b. guarding against thieves.
   c. spreading honey among the crops.
   d. making hives in the ground.

/4

Warm-Up

14   Trees Tell About Climates of the Past

Name _____

Trees store information about the climate. Scientists study the rings of preserved kauri trees. The ancient logs are up to 12 feet wide. Some of them are 130,000 years old. The trees lived for 2,000 years. They are in New Zealand's peat bogs. Wide ring widths show cool, dry summers. Tree rings tell how much carbon was in the air, too. Scientists often check 20 trees to be sure of their conclusions.

In Canada, scientists use tree rings to find past temperatures. Larger rings show warm temperatures. Trees in Canada do not live as long as those in warmer places. Once they get tall, wind and ice storms knock them down. Once a tree falls, it starts to rot. Then the data is harder to collect.

The pine trees in the southeastern United States hold hurricane data. One team looking at pine tree rings in Georgia found all known hurricanes in the area over the past 100 years. The team then checked old trees from nearby states. They found hurricane information for the past 227 years. How do they know? Hurricane rain has low amounts of oxygen-18. When wood tissue shows a sudden drop in oxygen-18, it proves a hurricane.

Climate researchers suspect that hurricanes are increasing. The only way to know is to have a long history of these storms.

Check Your Understanding

1. About how long do kauri trees live?
   a. 100 years
   b. 227 years
   c. 2,000 years
   d. 130,000 years

2. How do scientists use trees to gather hurricane data?
   a. They measure carbon content in trees.
   b. They count the number of rotting trees.
   c. They measure the size of the rings.
   d. They measure the oxygen-18 content in the rings.

3. What information is hardest to collect from trees?
   a. the amount of carbon in the air
   b. the average wind speed
   c. temperature
   d. rainfall

4. Why do trees in Canada live shorter lives than other trees?
   a. High winds and ice storms knock down the trees.
   b. They are a special, fast-growing species.
   c. Hurricanes deprive the trees of oxygen.
   d. They do not live in nutritious peat bogs.

/4

Warm-Up 15

Name _____

Snapping Turtles

Snapping turtles live in fresh water in North America, Central America, and parts of South America. There are two kinds. The common snapper lives in ponds from Canada to Ecuador. It grows to be 19 inches long. The alligator snapper lives in swamps in the central and southeastern United States. An alligator snapper is the biggest freshwater turtle in North America. It can grow more than three feet long and weigh more than 200 pounds! In some areas, people catch them and make turtle soup.

All snapping turtles have shells with rough edges. They have big heads with black eyes and a sharp beak. Snappers have strong jaws. They crush bones with one bite. A snapper cannot pull its head and legs inside its shell. So it uses its bite for defense. And it can swing its head around almost to its back legs if something grabs it from behind!

Snapping turtles eat small fish, frogs, snakes, other turtles, insects, snails, and baby geese and ducklings. They eat underwater plants, too. Snappers can live a long time. Some have lived 70 years. Scientists think they may be able to live 100 years.

There are fossils that prove that snapping turtles lived in Europe and Asia millions of years ago. Now snapping turtles only live in the Western Hemisphere. Why? Scientists are not sure.

Check Your Understanding

1. You could find a snapping turtle in
   a. a swamp in France.
   b. a pond in Ecuador.
   c. an ocean bay in Hawaii.
   d. a mountain stream in Africa.

2. If threatened, a snapping turtle is most likely to
   a. play dead.
   b. pull all its parts inside its shell.
   c. whip with its tail.
   d. bite with its jaws.

3. Which food is a snapping turtle least likely to eat?
   a. grasses
   b. pond plants
   c. snails
   d. frogs

4. How much longer is an alligator snapper than a regular snapper?
   a. just a little bit longer
   b. about twice as long
   c. about three times longer
   d. about four times longer

/4

Warm-Up

16   Eyelids

Name _____

Have you ever thought about your eyelids? Probably not. But they are an important part of your eye. They keep your eyes safe from being poked. Actually when your eyelashes detect anything near your eye, they automatically make your top and bottom eyelids close. It is a reflex to keep your eyes safe. Eyelids also let you blink. You blink many times each minute. Each blink bathes your eye in tears. Your tears contain proteins known as *lysozymes*. They kill bacteria. This keeps your eye clean.

Without eyelids, you would be blind within days. Your eyes would dry out, get infected, or be hurt by something getting into them. That's why most mammals, birds, reptiles, and amphibians have eyelids. However, all fish and most whales do not have eyelids. Dolphins are the exception. They swim fast. They need eyelids to protect their eyes against stuff floating in the water.

Reptiles have really cool eyelids. Snakes' eyelids are transparent. That means that you—and they—can see right through them. They keep their eyelids closed most of the time. Alligators have a third eyelid. It is clear and closes from back to front like a sliding-glass door. The third eyelid lets them lurk in muddy water and watch for prey.

Check Your Understanding

1. Which is *not* a benefit of blinking?
   a. Your eyesight keeps improving.
   b. Your eye is kept moist.
   c. Lysozymes kill bacteria.
   d. Your eye is protected from bright light.

2. With a reflex, your actions are
   a. automatic.
   b. slow.
   c. deliberate.
   d. uncoordinated.

3. Why can snakes keep their eyelids closed most of the time?
   a. They hunt using smell.
   b. They live in a dirty environment.
   c. They move very fast.
   d. They can see with their eyelids closed.

4. Which of the following animals is least likely to have eyelids?
   a. a frog
   b. a shark
   c. an iguana
   d. a turkey

/4

Warm-Up
17

Name _____

Solar Storms

You know that the sun **sustains** life on Earth. You know that you should never look right at the sun. It could blind you. But did you know that the sun has weather? It's nothing like the weather on Earth.

Our sun is a huge ball of burning plasma. Plasma is a state of matter where gas is superheated. Most of this plasma is hydrogen gas. The sun has an 11-year cycle. During its cycle, the sun has periods of major storm activity and minor storm activity. In the major storm part of the cycle, the sun has lots of solar flares. Solar flares are plasma eruptions. They shoot off the sun's surface. They cause solar wind. Just one average-sized solar flare releases enough energy to meet all the current power needs of the United States for 10,000 years!

The biggest solar plasma eruptions actually extend out into space like gigantic clouds. This solar wind shoots toward Earth at one million miles per hour. When strong solar winds hit Earth's atmosphere, the night sky glows. It comes from light reflecting off the ice at the Earth's North Pole. People call them the Northern Lights.

Check Your Understanding

1. The Northern Lights are caused by
   a. magnetic storms.
   b. solar wind.
   c. plasma.
   d. hydrogen gas.

2. An antonym for **sustains** is
   a. burns.
   b. chills.
   c. maintains.
   d. destroys.

3. Even small solar flares cause some
   a. solar wind.
   b. plasma.
   c. Northern Lights.
   d. hydrogen gas.

4. What is *not* a fact about the sun's weather cycle?
   a. Plasma heats up and cools down regularly.
   b. Each cycle lasts 11 years.
   c. The cycle has periods of major and minor activity.
   d. Most solar flares occur during periods of major activity.

/4

Warm-Up
18

Name _____

Breeding Bunnies

Most tame animals have been bred by people to look or act a certain way. This is why there are so many bunny breeds. People bred rabbits for different purposes. Angora rabbits were bred to have long hair. They do not need as much space and food as sheep, but their hair can make wool. First, people brushed the angora rabbits with a carding comb. This gently pulled out loose hair. Then the people took the hairs in the comb and spun it into yarn using a spinning wheel.

Other rabbits were raised for their pelts. Sewing many pelts together formed a fur coat. The Florida white rabbit was developed for medical research. A rabbit is enough like a human to use in experiments. Many large rabbits are raised for meat.

Rabbits always look like one or both of their parents. Sometimes people deliberately cross two different breeds to create a new breed. This happened with the Holland lop. A person took a Netherland Dwarf and mated it with a mini lop. The dwarf was a tiny bunny. The mini lop was small. The breeder wanted to get a tiny bunny with floppy ears. However, some of the babies looked like Netherland Dwarfs. Others looked like the mini lop. Breeders chose the smallest ones with lop ears and bred them together to make Holland lops.

Check Your Understanding

1. Rabbits have never been deliberately bred for
 a. meat.
 b. body size.
 c. ear type (lop or erect).
 d. foot size.

2. People use angora rabbit fur to
 a. make wool garments.
 b. made bandages.
 c. build rabbit nests for breeding colonies.
 d. use individual hair strands as wires in electronic items.

3. Which bunnies were bred together to make Holland lop rabbits?
 a. angora rabbits and mini lops
 b. angora rabbits and small Holland lops
 c. Netherland Dwarfs and mini lops
 d. Netherland Dwarfs and angora rabbits

4. Imagine a Holland lop bunny. What features would it almost certainly have?
 a. lop ears and a brown body
 b. lop ears and a small body
 c. small ears and a white body
 d. small ears and a small body

/4

Warm-Up
19

Name _____

Glaciers

Glaciers are gigantic sheets of ice. They **alter** Earth's surface. How? These slow-moving ice sheets keep water from draining away, forming lakes. Rivers change their courses to flow along the ice edges. Rain or snow falls on the glaciers. That water freezes and adds to its weight. The heavy weight can push down Earth's crust as much as 1,000 feet. The continent of Antarctica is almost completely underwater because of the weight of its thick glaciers!

The freezing and thawing of glaciers causes erosion of the rocks under and near the ice sheet. These loose rock pieces get dragged along. They scratch deep grooves into the land. This can turn V-shaped mountain valleys into wider, deeper U-shaped valleys. As glacier ice melts, it drops pieces of rock and soil. This forms a series of hills or ridges.

Half of the world's glaciers are in Alaska. Glaciers cover much of Greenland and almost all of Antarctica, too. However, many glaciers are melting due to global warming. Glacier National Park is in Montana. In the mid 1800s, it had 150 different glaciers. Now just 25 remain. Experts fear even those will be gone by 2030.

Check Your Understanding

1. Glaciers often change
   a. the length of an ice age.
   b. Earth's orbit around the sun.
   c. the temperature at the North Pole.
   d. the course of rivers.

2. A synonym for **alter** is
   a. damage.
   b. cool.
   c. change.
   d. create.

3. A glacier moving across land is most like
   a. a whittling knife carving a chunk of wood.
   b. a ship moving through big waves.
   c. a chain saw cutting down a tree.
   d. the damage caused by a tornado.

4. Picture a V-shaped mountain valley. Do you think a glacier formed it?
   a. No, because the valley would be more U-shaped if a glacier had formed it.
   b. No, because glaciers never affect valleys.
   c. Yes, glaciers have made all the valleys on Earth.
   d. Yes, glaciers often left this type of valley as they retreated.

/4

Name _____

20   Geothermal Energy

Earth has hot, melted rock miles below its surface. Right above this melted rock is a layer of hot, solid rocks. In some places, this heated layer lies close to the surface. People have found out how to use it to make electric power. They use geothermal energy. *Geo* stands for Earth. *Thermal* stands for heat.

In 1904, the first geothermal power station was built. People found a place in Italy where steam rose from the ground. They trapped the steam. They sent it through pipes to turbines. The turbines spun, which made electric power.

In most places, steam does not come up on its own. So people pump water down to the hot rocks. About two-thirds of the water flows out into cracks in the rocks. The other one-third returns as steam to drive the turbines.

There are five geothermal power plants in Iceland. One-fourth of the nation's power is made this way. Plus, 87 percent of the buildings in Iceland are heated with geothermal energy. The nation hopes to one day use geothermal for all its energy needs.

Geothermal energy is renewable. It will never run out. Best of all, it does not pollute the air, land, or water. People hope to find more places and better ways to harness geothermal power.

Check Your Understanding

1. What happens last when making geothermal electricity?
   a. Hot rocks heat water.
   b. Steam drives turbines.
   c. Water is pumped down to a layer of hot rocks.
   d. Water turns into steam.

2. Geothermal energy
   a. is nonrenewable.
   b. can be tapped into anywhere on Earth.
   c. pollutes groundwater.
   d. does not cause any pollution.

3. Another good title for this passage would be
   a. "Making Electricity from Earth's Heat."
   b. "Using Steam Turbines."
   c. "Making Power the Hard Way."
   d. "Italians Build First Geothermal Power Station."

4. About how long ago was the first geothermal power plant built?
   a. 5 years
   b. 87 years
   c. 100 years
   d. 160 years

/4

Warm-Up

21   Turning Soda Bottles into Blankets

Name _____

Every day there is less space on Earth for trash. Yet every day we make more trash. What can we do? We must recycle most of our trash. Recycling means that the trash will be made into something useful instead of put into a landfill.

Recycling helps Earth and saves space in trash dumps. Half of everything that we put into landfills could be recycled instead. In fact, most things made of paper, metal, aluminum, glass, and plastic can be recycled.

Paper can be ground up and made into new paper. Some brands of toilet tissue are made of recycled paper. Steel and aluminum cans can be melted down and made into new cans. The same is true of glass. This can be done over and over again. Recycling doesn't take as much energy as making things from scratch. So we can use less of Earth's fuel resources.

Plastic soda, water, and laundry detergent bottles can be recycled. They can be made into fleece blankets, park benches, fences, playgrounds, and lumber. Some people call plastic the "wood" of the future. Things made of plastic will last about 400 years—even outside in the weather. No wood can do that!

Check Your Understanding

1. The text's main idea is
   a. we should recycle everything that we can.
   b. we can build benches that last 400 years.
   c. how to use old newspapers.
   d. cans should be melted.

2. Which event occurs last?
   a. The can is put into a recycling bin.
   b. The can is melted down so it can be reused.
   c. A steel can gets filled with corn.
   d. A person uses the corn in the can.

3. What will happen if people begin to recycle all that they can?
   a. More of Earth's resources will be used up.
   b. Things will cost less money.
   c. Trash dumps will fill up faster.
   d. Trash dumps won't fill up so fast.

4. Plastic benches can last longer than wooden ones because plastic does not
   a. burn like wood.
   b. dissolve like wood.
   c. rust like wood.
   d. rot like wood.

/4

Warm-Up
22
Name _____

Using Two Legs Instead of Four

Sometimes apes walk on four legs. Sometimes they walk on two legs. Have you ever wondered why? The answer may surprise you. Apes live in Africa. Africa is the home of the Sahara Desert. It is the biggest hot desert on Earth. Africa is also the home of the Serengeti Plain. It is one of the largest grasslands on Earth.

However, long ago, Africa was neither dry nor covered in long grasses. It had forests, lakes, rivers, and streams. Today, apes walk on two legs on land only about 6 percent of the time. But the moment they step into water, they walk on two legs 100 percent of the time. Scientists believe that this is because long ago, their ancestors had to deal with an environment that was much wetter than the one of today.

Why did apes ever enter the water at all? Perhaps they needed to cross streams or rivers to get away from predators. Maybe they needed to do it to reach better food sources. We don't know for sure. No matter what their reason, they found that wading on all fours was risky. It too often led to drowning. Wading on two feet kept their noses and mouths above the water. Today, wading is an instinct for apes.

Check Your Understanding

1. The modern African climate differs from the ancient African climate because it is
   a. warmer.
   b. wetter.
   c. drier.
   d. colder.

2. Why is wading better than walking on four legs in the water?
   a. The apes are less apt to cut all their feet on sharp, submerged rocks.
   b. The apes are less vulnerable to predators.
   c. The apes can fish when they have free hands.
   d. The apes are less likely to drown.

3. What two landmarks can you find in Africa?
   a. the Sahara Desert and the Amazon rain forest
   b. the Sahara Desert and the Serengeti Plain
   c. Mount Everest and the Amazon rain forest
   d. Mount Everest and the Serengeti Plain

4. An ape will always walk on two legs when
   a. stepping into water.
   b. running in a rainstorm.
   c. crossing a grassy field.
   d. carrying its young.

/4

Warm-Up

Name _____

23   Exciting News About Stem Cells

Our bone marrow makes new stem cells all the time. These cells can turn into any kind of cell. They respond to signals called growth factors. They tell the stem cells to turn into bone, blood, or tissue cells. This can help people to heal. First, doctors remove stem cells from a person's bone. They inject these stem cells into the person's wound. The growth factors tell them to turn into the cells needed to heal the injury.

Doctors have made biodegradable scaffolds. These scaffolds break down naturally as healthy new tissue grows in its place. Scaffolds let blood cells bring oxygen to the stem cells as they regrow tissue. Dr. Stephen Badylak had a patient who cut off the tip of his finger. The doctor used skin from a pig bladder as a scaffold. He put it on the man's finger. Then, he added some of the man's stem cells to the scaffold. In eight weeks, the fingertip regrew!

Dr. Anthony Atala has made human bladders using stem cells. These new bladders are working inside people's bodies. The people's bodies may have rejected a donor's organ. Since their own stem cells made the bladders, their bodies accepted them.

Doctors hope that one day stem cells may treat diabetes, strokes, and liver disease. They may help people with spinal cord injuries, heart disease, cancer, and other deadly illnesses.

Check Your Understanding

1. How do stem cells work?
    a. They act like biodegradable scaffolds.
    b. Scientists can use them to replace of any type of cell.
    c. The body sends them signals to turn into a specific kind of cell.
    d. They prevent the body from rejecting a donor organ.

2. To help heal a person's wound, a biodegradable scaffold
    a. flows in the blood stream.
    b. allows blood to deliver oxygen to cells.
    c. replaces the body's natural tissue.
    d. holds a wound in place until it heals.

3. What disease will stem cells probably *not* be able to treat?
    a. cancer   c. diabetes
    b. liver disease   d. the flu

4. What human body part creates new stem cells?
    a. the bladder   c. bone marrow
    b. the liver   d. the heart

/4

Warm-Up 24

Name _____

Animal Instincts

Some animal behaviors come from learning and reasoning. But much of animal behavior comes from instincts. Instinctive behavior comes from reflexes and the urge to survive and reproduce. Every newborn human has reflexes. Reflexes are automatic. There is no thought involved. For example, if you pick up something that's hot, you will immediately put it down or drop it. You don't think about it. No one tells you to do it. The pain message doesn't even make it to your brain before you react! Your spinal cord triggers your reflex reaction to pain.

Every animal wants to stay alive. When an animal feels fear, it fights or flees. To protect her pups, a mother walrus will attack a polar bear. A squirrel will run up a tree to **elude** a fox.

Species would die off without the urge to reproduce. This instinct causes animals to mate. Some animals, like birds, have an instinct to care for their young, too. Birds sit on their eggs until they hatch. Then they bring food to the babies. They chase away predators from the nest. Mammals take care of their young, too. Most amphibians and reptiles do not.

Check Your Understanding

1. Read all of the statements. Decide what happens third.
   a. The polar bear goes away.
   b. The polar bear tries to snatch the infant.
   c. The mother walrus attacks the polar bear with her tusks.
   d. A polar bear sees a baby walrus.

2. A synonym for **elude** is
   a. escape.
   b. attack.
   c. trick.
   d. scare.

3. What is an example of a human reflex?
   a. giggling
   b. sneezing
   c. scratching
   d. sleeping

4. Picture a rabbit hopping into traffic on a busy street. The rabbit is most apt to
   a. leap up on a car.
   b. sit still and hope the cars don't hit it.
   c. run away from the cars.
   d. roll over and play dead.

/4

Warm-Up

25 Volcanic Eruptions

Earth's crust is like a giant cracked eggshell. Tectonic plates are the huge pieces of this shell. Volcanoes happen along the cracks between these plates. Big eruptions occur when pressure builds up inside a volcano. When a volcano erupts, magma (melted rock) from deep within Earth spills out. When it flows onto Earth's surface, it is called lava. Lava flows toward the lowest point. It covers everything in its path.

A volcano doesn't just spew lava. Big chunks of solid rock called volcanic bombs may shoot into the air. Volcanoes release clouds of ash and toxic gases, too. If these gases stay close to the ground, they kill living things. Ash can stay in the air for a long time before it falls. In 2010, a volcano in Iceland erupted for the first time since 1821. It sent so much ash into the air that many airports in Europe were closed for a week.

Earth has about 500 active land volcanoes. An active volcano has steam and gases coming from small vents all the time. Seven land volcanoes erupt 24 hours a day. Lava, steam, and gases escape. Hawaii, Italy, and Japan each have at least one. In Fortuna, Costa Rica, people have built restaurants near an active volcano. Diners sit at the windows. They watch Arenai. It is the second-most-active volcano in the world. It is always erupting.

Check Your Understanding

1. Imagine that you are running away from an erupting volcano. What is *not* falling from the sky?
a. toxic gas
b. hot rocks
c. ash
d. tectonic plates

2. Volcanoes erupt because
a. pressure builds up beneath them.
b. too much rock melts underneath the surface.
c. the tectonic plates are breaking apart.
d. they are on a schedule based on the rock cycle.

3. About how many active land volcanoes does Earth have?
a. 7
b. 13
c. 210
d. 500

4. What is the least common way for a volcano to kill a living thing?
a. by burying it in lava
b. by crushing it with volcanic bombs
c. by causing an airplane to crash
d. by smothering it with toxic gas

/4

Warm-Up
26   Live a Green Lifestyle

Name _____

With all the news reports about global warming, you may feel down. You may think there's nothing you can do to help. But that's not true. Earth's future depends on you! Start living green today.

How? Don't let the water run while you brush your teeth. Just doing that will save 240 gallons of water a month. Put everything that you can in your recycle bin. Just 40 percent of glass jars and bottles are recycled. The ones that end up in the dump never break down. Those resources are lost *forever*. Glass can be recycled over and over. And each recycled glass bottle saves enough energy to light a 100-watt bulb for 4 hours.

One-third of all the stuff in most U.S. landfills is packing material. Break down cardboard boxes and recycle them. Recycling one ton of cardboard saves 17 trees. Each year those 17 trees take 250 pounds of carbon dioxide from the air. That is one of the gases causing global warming.

Recycling newspapers is important. It takes 500,000 trees to make one week's Sunday newspapers printed in the United States. It should take none. Newspapers can be made from recycled newspapers. The more paper you recycle, the fewer trees will be cut down. Recycle plastic, too. Just half of the plastic bottles made in the U.S. are recycled.

Check Your Understanding

1. What is the main point of this passage?
   a. Global warming is a threat.
   b. Paper and plastic are recyclable.
   c. We can save trees by recycling.
   d. We should conserve Earth's resources.

2. Which step happens first in cardboard recycling?
   a. People collect scrap paper to recycle.
   b. Companies buy boxes made of recycled cardboard.
   c. A recycling plant makes new cardboard boxes from the scrap paper.
   d. More trees live longer and remove carbon dioxide from the air.

3. Why is it important to recycle glass?
   a. The world is running out of glass.
   b. Glass in landfills causes global warming.
   c. Making new glass requires a lot of energy.
   d. Trees are cut down to make new glass.

4. How many times can glass be recycled?
   a. once
   b. twice
   c. until it's broken in pieces
   d. There's no limit.

/4

Name _____

Understanding Hemispheres

The equator is an imaginary line. It runs around Earth's middle. Above the equator is the Northern Hemisphere. Below the equator is the Southern Hemisphere.

Earth spins on its axis. (It's another imaginary line.) Earth tilts on its axis as it orbits the sun. So at different times of the year, each hemisphere is closer to the sun. When the Northern Hemisphere tips toward the sun, it gets more light and warmth than the Southern Hemisphere. When the Southern Hemisphere tips toward the sun, it gets more light and warmth than the Northern Hemisphere. This is why the seasons in the Northern Hemisphere are the exact opposite of those in the Southern Hemisphere. On the first day of winter in North America, it is the first day of summer in South America.

There are no seasons along the equator. The weather is warm all the time. The farther a place is from the equator, the colder it gets. That's why Canada gets colder than Mexico. Lines of latitude tell how far a place is from the equator. This means that 30 degrees North latitude (Egypt) and 30 degrees South latitude (South Africa) are the same distance from the equator. They are just in different hemispheres. Places that are the same distance from the equator have similar seasons.

Check Your Understanding

1. What causes the seasons to change?
   a. Earth moves closer to the sun in the winter.
   b. Latitudes change throughout the year.
   c. Each hemisphere gets more exposure to the sun at different times in the year.
   d. Earth orbits the sun.

2. It is the first day of spring in the Southern Hemisphere. What is it in the Northern Hemisphere?
   a. the first day of spring   c. the first day of fall
   b. the first day of summer   d. the first day of winter

3. The nation of Kenya lies on the equator. You can conclude that it
   a. is completely in the Northern Hemisphere.   c. has changing seasons.
   b. is completely in the Southern Hemisphere.   d. does not have changing seasons.

4. Australia is the same distance from the equator as the state of Georgia. You can conclude that the
   a. seasons are similar in each place (mild or pronounced).
   b. seasons are the same (winter at the same time of year).
   c. weather is the same in both places.
   d. line of latitude for both is 30 degrees North.

/4

Warm-Up
28   Using Waste to Make Electricity

Biomass energy comes from plant matter or animal waste. The Netherlands has Earth's biggest biomass power plant. It uses chicken waste to make electric power. First the waste from 100,000 chickens is burned. This heats water. The water turns into steam. It spins turbines. This makes electric power for 10,000 homes! Minnesota built the first chicken-waste power plant in the United States. Now more power plants using chicken and pig waste are being built.

Greenhouse gases cause global warming. Burning biomass adds to greenhouse gases. But it adds less than burning fossil fuels. Fossil fuels formed from huge numbers of dead plants and animals. They were compressed over millions of years. If you cut down and burn a tree, you release carbon that was trapped recently. But if you burn a lump of coal, you release carbon from many trees that was trapped millions of years ago. That's why burning 20 pounds of coal puts 50 pounds of carbon into the air.

Burning animal waste helps global warming, too. Why? Leaving animal waste to rot produces methane. It is the worst greenhouse gas. It traps 20 times more heat than carbon dioxide. The methane in animal waste breaks down when it's burned. It turns into carbon dioxide and hydrogen.

Check Your Understanding

1. What step happens second when turning animal waste into electrical power?
   a. Turbines spin.
   b. Electrical power travels through wires to homes.
   c. Chicken waste is burned.
   d. Water turns into steam.

2. Which item contains the most carbon?
   a. 10 pounds of lumber
   b. 10 pounds of coal
   c. 10 pounds of cotton socks
   d. 10 pounds of water

3. How does burning animal waste help the environment?
   a. It is less damaging to the atmosphere than burning coal.
   b. Burning waste releases methane, which is safer than carbon dioxide.
   c. It cleans up all the animal waste.
   d. You need to burn less animal waste than coal to make the same amount of power.

4. A good place to build a biomass plant is near
   a. coal mines.
   b. a dump.
   c. chicken farms.
   d. a coal-burning power plant.

/4

Warm-Up 29

Name _____

Solar Energy

In one hour, more solar energy bathes Earth than the amount of energy used by the whole world last year. So why can't the sun provide all the energy we need? Actually, the sun could do so. But we need to capture it and store it. So far we don't know how to do either in the most effective way. Scientists are working on these issues.

Most solar energy comes from Concentrating Solar Power systems. They use lenses or mirrors to focus sunlight into one beam. This concentrated ray of light heats water. The water turns into steam. It spins turbines inside a power plant. This creates electric power.

Many of us use solar energy in small ways. We may have solar calculators and watches. We see solar cells used in streetlights and in the small lamps along sidewalks in people's yards. In watches and calculators, the solar power gets used right away. For the others, it is stored in a battery. Then it is used during darkness.

We need a good way to store solar energy. Otherwise, there are limits to its usefulness. Less sunlight falls in an area during its winter months. That's when energy is needed to heat buildings. Also, we need energy 24 hours a day. Since the sun does not shine at night, no solar energy is made then.

Check Your Understanding

1. Every _____, more solar energy shines on Earth than the amount of energy used worldwide in a year.
- a. minute
- b. hour
- c. day
- d. week

2. In a Concentrated Solar Power system, which step happens third?
- a. A single beam of sunlight heats water.
- b. Steam gets generated.
- c. Turbines spin.
- d. Mirrors concentrate rays of sunlight.

3. The most solar energy can be collected
- a. at night.
- b. on a cloudy day.
- c. on a clear day.
- d. on a rainy day.

4. In the western part of the United States, there are "sun farms" with rows of solar collectors. Each farm's location is chosen because
- a. the region is very flat.
- b. few wind storms occur in the area.
- c. the land is useless for other purposes.
- d. a lot of sunlight typically falls in the area.

/4

Warm-Up
30

Name _____

Adapting to Global Warming

Global warming is a reality. The planet is heating up. Polar ice is melting. As that ice melts, sea levels will slowly rise. This will occur around the world. People are taking steps to prepare for higher sea levels.

Boston has raised a sewage treatment plant. This will keep it from flooding. New York City plans to do the same. California has changed the water-control gates around the Sacramento River Delta. This was done to keep out saltwater when the sea level rises. Irrigation ditches carry water to crops. If saltwater mixed into the fresh water in those ditches, it would hurt or kill crops.

The United States isn't the only nation getting ready for rising sea levels. England has spent half a billion dollars. It used the funds to improve its Thames River flood control. Bangladesh is building flood control levees. All new buildings in that nation must be built on stilts. The Netherlands is upgrading its flood control dikes. Singapore is making its canals wider and deeper. This way they can hold more water.

In Canada, scientists have taken seeds from trees. These trees stand in British Columbia's cool rain forests. They are planting them in the ponderosa pine forests of Idaho. They want to be sure that the tree species does not die out.

Check Your Understanding

1. What is the text's main idea?
   a. Sea levels will slowly rise as glaciers melt.
   b. Nations are preparing for the effects of global warming.
   c. Global warming is a reality.
   d. Global warming could kill Canadian trees.

2. In this text, what things are mentioned in response to global warming?
   a. ways to cool the environment
   b. ways to prevent global warming
   c. ways to raise the sea level
   d. ways to prevent flooding

3. Scientists are working to protect tree species by
   a. allowing saltwater into irrigation ditches.
   b. planting seeds in new areas.
   c. upgrading flood-control dikes.
   d. widening canals.

4. What step has California taken due to global warming?
   a. The state has upgraded its flood-control dikes.
   b. The state has widened its irrigation canals.
   c. The state has changed water-control gates.
   d. The state has planted crops in new areas.

/4

From the Past

Warm-Up
1

Name _____

Where Did Everyone Go?

A ghost town is a place that is abandoned. No one lives there. Buildings, roads, and furniture were left behind. Over time, the buildings fall down. The roads get overgrown. It looks spooky. People may have left due to sickness or a war. Most often, they went to find better opportunities.

There are ghost towns all over the world. The American West has hundreds of them. One of the most famous is Bodie, California. It was built in 1870 near gold mines. By 1940, the gold was gone, so everyone left. The buildings still stand. Some even have dusty furniture and old canned food on shelves.

Eight hundred years ago, Native Americans called the Anasazi lived in the American southwest. Their land was very dry. They dug ditches that provided water to their crops. They built homes in the side of cliffs. Their homes were so well made that many of them still stand today. No one knows what became of them. They just vanished about 600 years ago. Their villages show no signs of a war, and they left no graves to indicate there was a serious illness.

The town of Serjilla in Syria was abandoned more than 800 years ago. The empty houses are still there today. They were built of stone. They break down slowly. No one knows why the people left.

Check Your Understanding

1. About how long ago did the Anasazi disappear?
   a. 370 years
   b. 400 years
   c. 600 years
   d. 800 years

2. What caused a whole town to spring up in Bodie, California?
   a. a gold mine
   b. a silver mine
   c. a diamond mine
   d. the transcontinental railroad

3. What is the name of the town deserted more than 800 years ago?
   a. Anasazi
   b. Serjilla
   c. Syria
   d. Bodie

4. What is the most likely reason why the Anasazi left their homes?
   a. A flash flood drowned them all.
   b. They didn't like their homes.
   c. They lost a war and were taken captive.
   d. Their crops failed due to a lack of rain.

/4

Warm-Up 2

Did George Washington Fight at Gettysburg?

Name _____

The Civil War's most deadly battle took place in 1863. Almost 50,000 men died or were hurt. (Many of the injured later died.) It was fought in the heat of July. It happened in Gettysburg, Pennsylvania.

The Union troops of the 20th Maine **regiment** were low on bullets. They were losing. Then, just when they had used up the last of their gunpowder, they say the ghost of George Washington appeared. He rode Blue Skin, one of his favorite horses. He did not speak. He raised his arm and gave the command for the men to charge. The men obeyed. They ran down the hill into deadly fire. Dozens of bullets struck the man and his horse. Still they raced toward the rebels. The Confederate troops turned and ran!

As a result of this charge, the Union kept Little Roundtop. Had it fallen into rebel hands, the Union would have lost the battle, and perhaps the war. Hundreds of troops on both sides saw the ghost. General Oliver Hunt reported the incident to Lincoln's war secretary.

Washington had lived in Virginia. During the War, it was a rebel state. Why would he help the Union Army? Perhaps the first president wanted the nation to stay united. Maybe it was because he disliked slavery.

Check Your Understanding

1. What was the name of one of George Washington's favorite horses?
   a. Blue Skin
   b. Thunder
   c. Lightning
   d. Blue Sky

2. The Civil War's deadliest battle occurred in
   a. Maine.
   b. Pennsylvania.
   c. Virginia.
   d. Washington.

3. The Confederate troops were also called
   a. Union forces.
   b. Roundtops.
   c. Yankees.
   d. Rebels.

4. A **regiment** is a(n)
   a. Army doctor.
   b. battlefield.
   c. group of soldiers.
   d. charge during a battle.

/4

Name _____

3   Iceboxes: The First Refrigerators

Before there were refrigerators, there were iceboxes. An icebox was like a cabinet. It had a top shelf, where a large block of ice sat. In the bottom part, food was kept on shelves. The cool air from the ice block moved down into this area and kept the food cool.

Where did the ice come from? In the winter, ice was cut from lakes. The huge blocks went by horse and sleigh (and later by rail car) to large brick warehouses. The walls of these warehouses were thick to keep out heat from outdoors. The blocks of ice were stacked close together. They were covered with straw, too. This helped to keep them from melting. As they were needed, the ice blocks were cut into smaller chunks. Then, they went to each home by horse and wagon. (In the 1920s, trucks started to do the deliveries.)

Of course no one has an icebox today. A compressor cools heated air and uses it to cool things inside a refrigerator. In 1834, Jacob Perkins put a compressor on an icebox. But, since it had to be cranked by hand, it didn't catch on. By 1913, electric power could run the compressor. But it was too noisy. In 1934, General Electric built the first practical refrigerator. It took about another 10 years before most families could afford one.

Check Your Understanding

1. Inside the ice warehouse, with what were the ice blocks covered?
   a. towels
   b. bricks
   c. straw
   d. lumber

2. In what year did Jacob Perkins add a compressor to an icebox?
   a. 1834
   b. 1913
   c. 1934
   d. 1944

3. Where was the ice block placed in a person's home?
   a. underneath the icebox
   b. on the top shelf of the icebox
   c. on the middle shelf of the icebox
   d. on the bottom shelf of the icebox

4. Which person must have paid the most for blocks of ice?
   a. one living in Alaska
   b. one living in Maine
   c. one living in Ohio
   d. one living in Florida

/4

Name _____

The U.S. Civil War

Slavery was once part of the American culture. It seems hard to believe, but back then, people thought it was okay. It was how things had always been done. Even great men in our history, like George Washington and Thomas Jefferson, had slaves. However, these slaves were not mistreated and were set free once their owners died.

Abolitionists wanted to end slavery. They worked to convince Americans that one human being should not own another. At last the people in the North agreed. But those in the South did not. That's why the U.S. Civil War was fought. The South wanted things to go on as they always had. The plantations in the South were huge

farms. Many slaves worked in the fields. The plantation owners said their farms had to have free labor. Without it, they would not survive.

The Southern states withdrew from the Union. They announced they were another nation. They did this in order to have slaves. U.S. President Abraham Lincoln said the states could not leave the Union. This led to the Civil War, which lasted five long, bloody years. When it ended, the nation was reunited. All the slaves were set free. But it took a long time to change how some of the Southerners viewed African Americans.

Check Your Understanding

1. Who was the president during the Civil War?
   a. Thomas Jefferson
   b. Abraham Lincoln
   c. George Washington
   d. The passage does not say.

2. An **abolitionist** is a person who is
   a. for women's rights.
   b. trying to restore land to Native American tribes.
   c. against slavery.
   d. a civil war soldier.

3. Which of these events happened first?
   a. Slaves worked on Southern plantations.
   b. The Southern states withdrew from the Union.
   c. The U.S. Civil War was fought.
   d. Abolitionists protested.

4. Why did the Southern states leave the Union?
   a. They wanted to start a war with the Northern states.
   b. They wanted to free the slaves on plantations.
   c. They did it to protest against the abolitionists.
   d. They wanted their citizens to own slaves.

/4

Warm-Up
5

Name _____

The Montgomery Bus Boycott

The Civil Rights Movement caused changes in America. On December 1, 1955, the first major event took place in Montgomery, Alabama.

When the buses filled up, people thought African Americans should stand up. They had to give their seats to white riders. Rosa Parks was an African American woman. On that date, Parks did not give up her seat. A white man could not sit down. Because of this, the police put her in jail!

Rosa worked with a civil rights group. Jo Ann Robinson was another local activist. She was the Women's Political Council president. She had a plan. Jo Ann stayed up all night. She made 35,000 fliers. She sent them to every African American in the city. The fliers said not to ride the buses. Jo Ann meant for the **boycott** to last one day. Instead, it lasted a whole year.

This was a peaceful protest. African Americans from all over the city worked together. Not one of them set foot on a bus. The bus company started to go broke. It had to get the people back on the buses. So, the law changed. Anyone could sit wherever he or she chose on a bus. No one was forced to give up a seat for another person.

Check Your Understanding

1. How many African Americans rode the buses during the Montgomery boycott?
   a. none
   b. 195
   c. 350
   d. 635

2. How long did Jo Ann Robinson expect the boycott to last?
   a. 1 day
   b. 1 week
   c. 1 month
   d. 1 year

3. When a person participates in a **boycott**, he or she will
   a. make fliers and pass them out.
   b. refuse to give up his or her seat on a bus.
   c. march in a protest.
   d. not buy or use a product or a service.

4. Why was the bus boycott so effective?
   a. It made many local businesses lose a lot of income.
   b. The fliers Jo Ann made persuaded lawmakers to change the law.
   c. The bus company influenced the lawmakers to change the law.
   d. The bus company needed African American drivers.

/4

Warm-Up 6

How U.S. Libraries Began

Name _____

Do you like going to your school or public library? You know that you can borrow books and other things. It's free. You only have to pay if you lose an item or bring it back late. Public libraries have made knowledge available to all people.

It wasn't always this way. Years ago, just the rich had libraries. They had rooms in their homes that held thousands of books. But they only lent them to friends. A few towns had libraries. But a person had to pay to borrow the books. Colleges had libraries, too. Only their students could use them.

When the United States was a new nation, it created the Library of Congress in Washington, D.C. It was for the use of the members of Congress. However, the British burned the city in 1812. This wiped out the collection. A new building was built. But there were no books. So Thomas Jefferson sold his own personal library to fill the shelves. Now the Library of Congress is the largest library on Earth.

Andrew Carnegie was a very rich American. He wanted everyone to be able to use a library. So, in 1919, he gave the funds to build 1,700 public libraries. They went up all over the United States.

Check Your Understanding

1. Some of the U.S. public libraries were built with money given by
   a. colleges.
   b. Thomas Jefferson.
   c. Andrew Carnegie.
   d. a foreign government.

2. If people do not have a chance to read books, they may
   a. not get to learn new things.
   b. get sick.
   c. find a better job.
   d. go to school.

3. Before there were public libraries,
   a. most people had access to books.
   b. colleges did not have libraries either.
   c. there were only a few books published.
   d. few people had access to books.

4. Which statement about the Library of Congress is false?
   a. It is the world's biggest library.
   b. Andrew Carnegie donated the money to build it.
   c. Thomas Jefferson used his own book collection to fill its shelves.
   d. It was once destroyed by the British.

/4

Warm-Up 7

Name _____

The Orphan Trains

An orphan is a child whose parents have died. In the late 1800s, many orphans lived in New York City. Thousands of children lived in the streets. They slept in boxes or under bridges. They begged or stole food.

Nuns started orphanages so these children could have food to eat. But there were more children than they could help. Charles Loring Brace believed that all of the children needed homes. In 1854, he came up with an idea to help both the children and the families who took them in. He decided to send the children out West on trains. Farm families could adopt the children. Farmers could usually feed another mouth. Many could use another pair of hands to help with the chores.

During the next 75 years, about 200,000 children rode these trains. A poster in each town on the railroad told people when the children would arrive. When the train pulled in, the children lined up on the station platform. The people who wanted a child chose one. The children who were not chosen got back on the train and went to the next town. Most of the children found parents who cared about them. They found love and a new life by riding the orphan train.

Check Your Understanding

1. About how many children went West on an orphan train?
   a. 200
   b. 2,000
   c. 20,000
   d. 200,000

2. What happened last?
   a. The child's parents passed away.
   b. The child was chosen by a farmer.
   c. The child lived on the streets.
   d. The child rode an orphan train.

3. How did people know when the orphan trains would arrive?
   a. The information was posted on the Internet.
   b. The nuns called families by phone to tell them.
   c. Posters were displayed with the information.
   d. The orphan trains arrived every other Monday.

4. You can tell that the orphan train idea
   a. was started by nuns.
   b. was not liked by Charles Brace.
   c. helped the nuns earn money for the orphanages.
   d. helped a lot of children have better lives.

/4

From the Past

Name _____

Warm-Up
8
Braille for the Blind

Louis Braille was born in 1809 able to see. But he had an accident when he was three years old. He was playing with a tool and stabbed himself in the eye. To make matters worse, he got an **infection** that spread to his good eye. Then he lost the vision in that eye, too.

When he was 10, he went to the world's first school for the blind. He learned to read books with raised letters. But the method used to make the books was expensive and took a lot of labor. The school had only 14 books. Louis knew there had to be a better way. When he was just 15, he invented Braille writing. The first Braille books were printed in 1829.

Braille is a writing system made up of patterns of raised dots inside cells. A blind person can run his or her finger across the dots and recognize the pattern. He or she can tell what each letter is by feeling it with a fingertip. There can be between two and six dots in one cell. Each cell represents a letter, a numeral, or a punctuation mark. Some frequently used words and letter combinations (such as *th*) have their own single cell patterns.

Braille is used to write many different languages, including Chinese. Now many books are on CD, allowing blind people to listen to them. However, Braille is still the way that most blind people read and write.

Check Your Understanding

1. Braille is used by people who
   a. cannot walk.
   b. are deaf.
   c. cannot move their fingers.
   d. are blind.

2. An **infection** is a(n)
   a. condition caused by germs.
   b. birth defect.
   c. serious injury.
   d. allergy that can kill a person.

3. Which event occurred last?
   a. Books for the blind were printed with raised letters.
   b. Louis went to school.
   c. Louis went blind in both eyes.
   d. Books for the blind were printed with Braille.

4. Which statement is false?
   a. Braille is a method for reading and writing.
   b. Braille is used to write Chinese.
   c. Now that there are books on CD, no one learns Braille.
   d. The letter combination *ch* has its own Braille cell pattern.

/4

Warm-Up 9

Name _____

The Invention of the Microwave Oven

Do you like to "zap" your food in the microwave? It is the easiest way for kids to cook. Actually, using a microwave is an easy way for anyone to cook. Yet the technology behind it was discovered by accident.

During Word War II, scientists used magnetrons. They are long tubes that produce microwaves. They wanted to improve radar. Dr. Percy Spencer was an engineer. He tested magnetron tubes. One day in 1946, he wanted a snack. He reached into his pocket. He had a candy bar in there. But what he found was a sticky mess. His candy bar had melted! But how? The magnetron tube must have melted his candy bar.

Percy put a bag of popcorn kernels near the tube. They started to pop! Next, he put an egg (in its shell) inside a pot. He cut a hole in the pot. He directed the magnetron beam at the hole. The egg exploded. He told his boss. His company, Raytheon, applied for a patent.

Within a year, Raytheon had made the first microwave oven. The Radarange was the size of a refrigerator! Only restaurants bought these ovens. In 1952, another company offered the first home microwave for $1,295. Today most cost less than $100. It took about 30 years before the ovens really caught on.

Check Your Understanding

1. The very first microwave ovens were purchased by
   a. the U.S. Army.
   b. restaurants.
   c. airlines.
   d. hospitals.

2. What happened to the egg in Dr. Spencer's experiment?
   a. It got so hot that it expanded.
   b. He hit it with the pot.
   c. It caught on fire.
   d. It crumbled into tiny pieces like sand.

3. What was the name of the first microwave oven?
   a. Magnetron
   b. Raytheon
   c. Spencerwave
   d. Radarange

4. Since the first home microwave came out, the price has dropped by about
   a. $100.
   b. $120.
   c. $1,200.
   d. $1,295.

/4

Warm-Up
10

Name _____

The World's First Robot and His Dog

The world's first voice-activated robot made his debut with his dog in 1939. That year Elektro the Moto-Man and his robot dog, Sparko, were the biggest hits in New York. The city hosted the World's Fair. People waited in line for eight hours. They wanted to see the large gold metal robot and his four-legged pal. Elektro was 7 feet tall. He weighed 265 pounds.

At that time, the nation was just coming out of the Great Depression. Westinghouse built the gentle giant and his pup to please the crowds. The World's Fair lasted for two years. Elektro and Sparko were the number one hit.

What could the duo do? Elektro moved his head and arms and blew up balloons.

He could walk and speak about 700 words. His "eyes" could tell the difference between red and green light. Sparko could bark, sit, and beg when given commands. The robots' operator was Marguerite Smith. She spoke commands into a telephone. The robots would respond to her voice. She had to say each word in a slow, stilted way.

Westinghouse kept improving Elektro. He went on a road tour around the nation. However, he was retired in the 1960s. Now he is being restored. He will be on display at the Mansfield Memorial Museum in Ohio. Would you like to meet him?

Check Your Understanding

1. Which event occurred third?
   a. Marguerite Smith operated Elektro at the World's Fair.
   b. Westinghouse created Sparko.
   c. Elektro will be on display at a museum.
   d. Elektro did a tour across the United States.

2. How many words could Elektro say?
   a. 265
   b. 700
   c. 900
   d. 1,960

3. The 1939 World's Fair was held in
   a. New York City, New York.
   b. St. Louis, Missouri.
   c. Mansfield, Ohio.
   d. Chicago, Illinois.

4. What was the name of Elektro's pet?
   a. Marguerite
   b. Robodog
   c. Moto-Man
   d. Sparko

/4

Warm-Up
11 How Plumbing Changed America

Name _____

Can you imagine life before plumbing? It was very different. Houses did not have sinks, showers, or toilets. Before building a home, you drilled to find water for a well. After you'd dug the well, you worked a pump to bring up the water. Every drop of water had to be carried into the house. If you wanted warm water for a bath, you heated it on the stove. When you needed a bathroom, you went to an outhouse.

By the 1940s, most Americans had indoor plumbing. Your plumbing system supplies clean water to the tub, shower, sinks, washer, and toilet. The clean water often comes from rivers and lakes. First, it goes through a water treatment plant that **purifies** the water. Then, the clean water flows through big pipes under the streets. Each house on the street connects to the pipe.

A different set of larger pipes takes away used water. Wastewater from sinks, tubs, and toilets leaves through these sewage pipes. Sewage flows through underground pipes to a treatment plant. After the plant gets rid of bacteria, the water goes into a river or lake.

Indoor plumbing helped people live longer. They could keep themselves and their homes cleaner than ever before. This kept them healthier.

Check Your Understanding

1. Before houses had indoor plumbing, people got their clean water from a
   a. well.
   b. pipe.
   c. water treatment plant.
   d. ditch.

2. A synonym for **purifies** is
   a. changes.
   b. pumps.
   c. cleans.
   d. stirs.

3. Picture a bathroom. What does *not* use plumbing?
   a. the shower
   b. the sink
   c. the toilet
   d. the light

4. Why are clean water pipes narrower than sewage pipes?
   a. People don't need very much clean water.
   b. Clean water never contains solids.
   c. Clean water pipes are made of plastic.
   d. Clean water is heavier than sewage.

/4

Warm-Up

12

Name _____

Highway History

In Great Britain, drivers drive on the opposite side of the road from drivers in North America. Why? London Bridge was wide. But it had many buildings on it. In some spots, this made it as narrow as 12 feet. The bridge was the only way into London. As many as 75,000 people crossed every 24 hours! One day in 1625, a horse pulling a wagon died on the bridge. This blocked a narrow part. No one could get into or out of the city.

After that, the Lord Mayor of London made a law. Traffic coming into the city must stay on the left. Traffic leaving the city must stay on the right. Most nations settled by the British follow this plan. America was once a British colony.

So why the switch? To defy the British, the people began to drive on the opposite side. This was during the American Revolution. Everyone got used to it. The roads in Canada join the ones in the United States. So they follow the U.S. custom, too.

In the 1950s, President Eisenhower set up the U.S. interstate system of highways. He wanted to connect the whole nation. As a result, America has the most extensive highway system on Earth. President Eisenhower made a rule. On each interstate highway, one mile in every five miles had to be straight. Planes can use these sections for runways in war or emergencies.

Check Your Understanding

1. Why did the London leader create the first traffic law?
   a. A crowd of 75,000 people marched on his home, demanding he take action.
   b. He wanted to annoy the colonists living in America.
   c. He wanted people to stop putting buildings on London Bridge.
   d. A horse died and caused a traffic jam.

2. Bermuda is a nation that the British settled. In Bermuda, people
   a. do not drive.
   b. drive on the same side of the road as Americans.
   c. drive on the opposite side of the road from Americans.
   d. have no traffic laws.

3. Which nation has the world's most extensive highway system?
   a. the United States   c. Canada
   b. London   d. Great Britain

4. Why did the American colonists change the road traditions?
   a. They were angry with the British.
   b. They wanted to match the roads in Canada.
   c. They wanted to be different from other British colonies.
   d. They refused to follow any traffic laws.

/4

Warm-Up

13   The Buried Village of Ozette

Name _____

The Makah Native Americans live in what is now the state of Washington. For years they had villages along the coast. They had an oral story that told of a terrible storm. It caused a huge landslide that buried a whole village. This happened about 500 years ago. No one knew where to look for the **entombed** village of Ozette. Some even doubted the story was true.

Then, in February 1970, a winter storm struck the coast. It caused giant waves, strong winds, and steady rain. The storm pounded the beach and cliffs. This caused another huge landslide. The next day, a hiker came across a paddle. It was sticking out of the mud.

When the mud buried Ozette, it was awful. Many homes and dozens of people were buried alive. However, the wet, oxygen-free conditions left lots of the things under the 10-foot-thick clay in great shape. Many were perfectly preserved. This is uncommon. Often, scientists figure out what a very old thing looked like from a few of its pieces or its impression left in clay. They found intact items at Ozette! They found harpoons, canoes, and whistles. They dug out combs, cedar ropes, and baskets.

Check Your Understanding

1. In February 1970, what old Native American object did a Washington hiker find in the mud?
   a. a basket and cedar rope
   b. a canoe
   c. a home
   d. a paddle

2. The word **entombed** means
   a. mysterious.
   b. ancient.
   c. buried.
   d. missing.

3. Why were people *not* sure the story was true before 1970?
   a. There had never been a landslide anywhere else.
   b. People enjoyed making up disaster stories.
   c. There was no evidence to prove it had happened.
   d. It's rare that a story passed down by word of mouth is ever true.

4. The same kind of natural disaster first destroyed and then led to the discovery of Ozette. What was the type of disaster?
   a. a landslide
   b. an earthquake
   c. a wildfire
   d. a flood

/4

Warm-Up

14

World War II Spies

Name _____

Spies are important during a war. They gather information called intelligence. A spy must always pose as if he or she were actually on the opposite side. So, for example, a Russian spy in World War II had to pretend he was German. In truth, he worked for the enemy. That's why it is dangerous to be a war spy. If you are caught, you could be killed.

Richard Sorge posed as a German news reporter in Japan. Japan was on the same side as Germany. But he was really a spy for Russia. He found out that Japan did not plan to attack Russia. He told Russia to move all its troops to fight the Germans. The Japanese discovered Richard and killed him. Some call him history's greatest spy.

A German spy family lived in Hawaii. They helped the Japanese attack Pearl Harbor. The Kuehns had a 17-year-old daughter, Susie. They had an 11-year-old son, Hans. Susie dated U.S. sailors. They told her all about their ships. Some took her little brother on a tour of the ships. The mother ran a beauty salon. She talked to sailors' wives. The father sent all the information to the Japanese embassy in Hawaii. He used a flashlight code. In response to their questions, he hung different kinds of clothes on the clothesline. After Pearl Harbor was bombed, the family was imprisoned.

Check Your Understanding

1. Which embassy was Mr. Kuehn contacting?
   a. Russian
   b. American
   c. Japanese
   d. German

2. Who posed as a German working in Japan?
   a. Hans Kuehn
   b. Richard Sorge
   c. Gretel Kuehn
   d. Susie Kuehn

3. What usually happened to a spy who was caught during a war?
   a. The person was forced to leave the country.
   b. The person was imprisoned until he or she wrote a letter of apology.
   c. The person spent the rest of his or her life at a work camp.
   d. The person was executed.

4. Which two nations were on the same side during World War II?
   a. Germany and Japan
   b. America and Germany
   c. Germany and Russia
   d. Russia and Japan

/4

Warm-Up
15   Inventions that Use Electricity

Name _____

Andrew Ure invented the thermostat in 1830. It controls your home's temperature. A thermostat is always mounted on an inside wall. That way the outside temperature does not affect it. How does it work? All metals expand when heated. They shrink when cooled. But they do so at different rates. A thermostat has a metal strip. It is made of copper and iron. Copper reacts to temperature changes more than iron does. It expands and shrinks more.

Ure took two long thin pieces of each metal. He welded them together. The metal strip curls one way when it is hot. It curls the other way when it is cooled. The strip touches a contact. It completes an electrical circuit. The circuit turns a heating or cooling system on or off.

In 1879, Thomas Edison invented the incandescent light bulb. It glowed as electricity passed through a filament. This kind of light bulb will burn your fingers after it has been on for a few minutes. That is because incandescent bulbs make light and heat.

In 1976, Ed Hammer invented compact fluorescent bulbs. They are more efficient. They produce light, but little heat. This means that they last longer and use less energy. In 2010, Australia outlawed incandescent bulbs. Its citizens must use compact fluorescent bulbs.

Check Your Understanding

1. In what year was the compact fluorescent bulb invented?
    a. 1830   c. 1976
    b. 1879   d. 2010

2. The two metals used in thermostats are copper and
    a. nickel.   c. iron.
    b. aluminum.   d. silver.

3. Which nation recently outlawed incandescent bulbs?
    a. France   c. the United States
    b. Australia   d. Austria

4. What makes a compact fluorescent bulb superior to an incandescent bulb?
    a. It eliminates the need for a thermostat in the house.
    b. It reduces the need for heating in the winter.
    c. It reduces the need for air conditioning in the summer.
    d. It produces just as much light using much less energy.

/4

Warm-Up

16 Skiing

Name _____

Do you like to ski? The oldest pair of skis we have is 5,000 years old. The ancient skis were found in a bog in Norway. The word ski comes from the Norse word for *stick of wood*. The first skis were not for going downhill fast. They were more like cross country skis. They helped people go from place to place in the winter.

Cave drawings prove that about 4,000 years ago, people in Sweden and Finland used skis. There are pictures of people on skis. In northern China, there are similar cave drawings. The Chinese say that their drawings are close to 10,000 years old.

About 2,000 years ago, the Romans invaded Finland. The Romans saw their skis. Then, as the Romans spread across Europe, skis went with them. However, skis didn't make it across the Atlantic. Then, about 170 years ago, people from Norway came to the United States. They brought skis with them.

In 1850, a new binding was made. It held skiers' feet in place without losing their skis. Soon after that, people began skiing downhill. Within a few years, racing began. Skiing became an Olympic sport in 1928.

Check Your Understanding

1. Skiing was invented as a(n)
   a. winter racing sport.
   b. way to get around.
   c. alternative to ice skating.
   d. way to keep runners in shape during winter.

2. The word *ski* comes from which language?
   a. Roman
   b. Finnish
   c. Norse
   d. Swedish

3. What do we know is a fact?
   a. People have been skiing for at least 5,000 years.
   b. People have been skiing for at least 10,000 years.
   c. Finnish immigrants brought skiing to the United States.
   d. From the start, people used skis for downhill racing.

4. About how long ago did skiing become an Olympic sport?
   a. 50 years
   b. 60 years
   c. 80 years
   d. 160 years

/4

Name _____

The Great Liberty Bell Adventure

The Liberty Bell was cast in Great Britain in 1751. It traveled by ship to Philadelphia, Pennsylvania. The first time it rang, it cracked! So the bell was melted down. It was recast in 1752. When it rang, it sounded awful! It was melted down again and recast in 1753. Then it was hung in the State House. It was rung to call people to meetings.

In September 1777, the American colonists were at war with Great Britain. The British were marching toward the city. The colonists knew that the troops would melt the one-ton bell. They would use the metal to make bullets to shoot them! A brave family named the Mickleys agreed to take the bell out of the city. The Mickleys had an 11-year-old son.

Because the bell filled their whole wagon, the Mickleys had to leave behind all they owned. They covered the bell in hay. After three days of travel, they reached the Zion Reformed Church in Northampton Town (now Allentown, Pennsylvania). They pulled up the floorboards and hid the bell beneath them. Then they nailed the boards back in place. The bell remained hidden there for a year.

Later, the Liberty Bell returned to the State House unharmed by its adventure. But in 1835, it cracked when it rang during a funeral. It has only been rung once since that time.

Check Your Understanding

1. Why did the Mickleys give up all their possessions?
   a. The bell took up all the space in their wagon.
   b. They had to leave town so fast that there was no time to pack their things.
   c. They wanted to buy all new things.
   d. They went to live in Zion Reformed Church, and it was fully furnished.

2. Which event occurred last?
   a. The Liberty Bell was hidden beneath the Zion Reformed Church.
   b. The Liberty Bell was cast in Philadelphia.
   c. The Liberty Bell was cast in Great Britain.
   d. The Liberty Bell cracked during a funeral.

3. If the Liberty Bell had fallen into British hands, it would have been
   a. made into ammunition for guns.   c. sent back to Great Britain.
   b. made into a cannon.   d. made into pots and pans for the army.

4. Leaders rang the Liberty Bell on July 4, 1776. Why?
   a. They told the people that Great Britain had declared war on America.
   b. They read aloud the Declaration of Independence to the people.
   c. They told the people that British had just surrendered, ending the American Revolution.
   d. They wanted people to decide whether the bell should be recast or not.

/4

Warm-Up

18   Massachusetts Promotes Education

Name _____

Do you like school? If so, then you like the state of Massachusetts. In the United States, it has had more education "firsts" than any other state. The Boston Latin School opened in 1635. It was the colonies' first public school. In 1642, Massachusetts was the first state to pass a law that children under the age of 11 had to go to school. In 1820, the first American high school opened. It was in Boston. Just four years later, a public high school just for girls opened its doors. In 1827, Massachusetts offered the first free public schools. Two years later, it had the first school for the blind.

The Massachusetts Board of Education first met in 1837. It is the nation's oldest state board of education. In 1846, a school in Quincy was the first to group students by grade level. Two years later, Boston had the first school for kids with learning problems. In 1853, Massachusetts was the first state to require gym classes. Seven years after that, the nation's first kindergarten opened in Boston.

Harvard University was the first college in America. And guess where it is? Cambridge, Massachusetts. It admitted its first students in 1636. Today it is one of the most famous colleges in the world.

Check Your Understanding

1. The nation's oldest state board of education first met in
    a. 1635.   c. 1827.
    b. 1642.   d. 1837.

2. Which event occurred last?
    a. Massachusetts had the first free public schools in America.
    b. The Boston Latin School held classes.
    c. Massachusetts started the first school for the blind.
    d. Massachusetts passed a law that children up to age 10 had to attend school.

3. Look at the passage title. You can tell that the word **promotes** means
    a. modifies.   c. discovers.
    b. encourages.   d. discourages.

4. You can conclude that
    a. no other state in the U.S. cares as much about education as Massachusetts does.
    b. Harvard University opened its doors before the Boston Latin School did.
    c. today children over the age of 11 do not have to attend school in Massachusetts.
    d. Quincy and Cambridge are cities in Massachusetts.

/4

Warm-Up
19

Name _____

Decoding Hieroglyphs

People have always had ideas that they wanted to share. The first people drew on cave walls. These pictures showed how to hunt deer. Later people around the world started to write down their ideas. Each group had a different way. People in the Middle East made marks in damp clay called *cuneiform.*

The ancient Egyptians used pictures called *hieroglyphs.* Each picture stood for a sound. We would not know how to read hieroglyphs if it wasn't for the Rosetta Stone, which was found by accident. In 1799, a French soldier tore down an old wall inside a fort in Egypt. Inside the wall, the soldier found an odd stone. The black slab had three languages carved on it. He showed it to his officer. The officer knew it was an important find. They carefully removed the stone from the wall. Then they turned the Rosetta Stone over to scholars.

Until that time no one knew how to read hieroglyphs, the language of ancient Egypt. The Rosetta Stone had the same message written in Greek and hieroglyphs. Many people knew Greek. They used their understanding of Greek to read the hieroglyphs. It took them 20 years before they understood all of the symbols.

Check Your Understanding

1. If the Rosetta Stone had never been uncovered, people would
   a. be able to read Egyptian hieroglyphs more accurately.
   b. have changed Egyptian hieroglyphs into letters.
   c. have not given Egyptian hieroglyphs another thought.
   d. probably not know how to read Egyptian hieroglyphs.

2. Why did the officer know the Rosetta Stone was important?
   a. He saw that the Rosetta Stone was old and had writing on it.
   b. The Rosetta Stone was made of gold.
   c. He had been sent to search for the Rosetta Stone.
   d. He knew how to read the hieroglyphs on the Stone.

3. The Rosetta Stone had the same message in three languages. Whoever made it
   a. wanted to cover the entire face of the Stone.
   b. knew that it would someday help people to decode hieroglyphs.
   c. wanted as many people as possible to be able to read it.
   d. knew that it would one day be buried in an old wall.

4. Which statement is false?
   a. Hieroglyphs and cuneiform are the same types of writing.
   b. The Rosetta Stone was discovered by accident.
   c. Our modern alphabet is not closely related to hieroglyphs.
   d. People in the Middle East wrote using cuneiform.

/4

Warm-Up 20

Canned Foods

Name _____

The French Emperor Napoleon was always fighting a war. He wanted to feed his troops easily. So, in 1800, he offered a prize. He would give 12,000 francs to anyone who could keep food fresh in a bottle or jar. It was a huge prize. It would be like offering $400,000 today. Many people tried. They did not succeed.

Then, a candy maker named Nicolas Appert figured out how to preserve soups, jams, and vegetables. He claimed the prize in 1809. In 1810, La Maison Appert opened. It was the first food-bottling factory. Appert filled thick, wide-mouth glass bottles with food. He put a cork in the top. Then, the bottles were wrapped in canvas. Last, he boiled the bottles for a long time.

A British man named Peter Durand used the same method to preserve food. But then he sealed it in tin cans. In 1813, a British factory started making canned foods. These foods were just for the British army.

Now here's the odd part. No one invented a can opener until 1858! For 45 years, the only way to open canned foods was with a hammer and a nail. The person tapped holes around the lid's edges. When there were enough holes, the lid could be lifted. Hungry people took a shortcut and used an ax!

Check Your Understanding

1. How long did it take someone to claim Napoleon's prize?
   a. 3 years
   b. 6 years
   c. 9 years
   d. 10 years

2. Which event occurred second?
   a. Peter Durand canned foods.
   b. Napoleon offered a prize.
   c. The can opener was invented.
   d. Nicolas Appert bottled foods.

3. How much time passed between the start of the British canned foods and the invention of the can opener?
   a. 4 years
   b. 5 years
   c. 45 years
   d. 54 years

4. How did the hungry troops open La Maison Appert's glass bottles?
   a. They hit them with a hammer.
   b. They removed the cork.
   c. They used a can opener.
   d. They unscrewed the metal cap.

/4

Warm-Up 21

Name _____

America's First Master Spy

George Washington was America's first master spy. He knew that his Continental Army was up against the world's strongest army. He knew that his men couldn't outfight the British. So he had to outsmart them. And it worked. Major George Beckwith was the head of the British spies. At the end of the American Revolution, he said, "Washington didn't outfight us. He out-spied us."

Washington's spy ring was called the Culper Gang. This group of men and women acted as if they were loyal to the British. That way the British spoke in front of them. Then, the spies sent Washington secret messages. They wrote in invisible ink between the visible lines in letters.

Washington had invented a stain that, when wiped on the papers, made this ink visible. Sending information this way meant that if the letters fell into British hands, they wouldn't know what they had. The gang also used a code based on letters and numbers. But this was more dangerous. It meant the sender and receiver needed a code book.

Lydia Darragh owned a tavern. She listened to the British plans. Then, she wrote on tiny notes and put them under the cloth-covered buttons on her son's coat. The boy walked to the American camp. Washington cut off his buttons. Then, he made sure that false battle plans fell into British hands.

Check Your Understanding

1. How did Lydia Darragh find out about British war plans?
   a. She listened to them talk in her tavern.
   b. She listened from behind a tree.
   c. She received notes from them underneath buttons.
   d. She could read invisible ink.

2. The head of the British spies was named George
   a. Washington.
   b. Beckwith.
   c. Culper.
   d. Darragh.

3. The invisible ink was clever because even if the British
   a. got the notes, they couldn't see the secret information.
   b. caught the boy, they wouldn't know about his buttons.
   c. got the notes, it would take them weeks to crack the secret code.
   d. caught Lydia Darragh, she did not know the names of others in the Culper Gang.

4. Washington wanted the British to have false battle plans so that they would not
   a. have enough troops in the correct location.
   b. have their own spies.
   c. have enough supplies.
   d. discover the Culper Gang's secret code.

/4

Amazing Ancient Structures

Ancient people created amazing structures even though they had limited tools and no machinery. Many of these works of art no longer exist. We know about them from things written at the time. King Nebuchadnezzar had the Hanging Gardens of Babylon built in 600 BCE as a gift for his wife. It had stone terraces 30 stories high. Masses of flowers were planted on each level. A sprinkling system brought water to the plants. It came from the Euphrates River.

Zeus was the most powerful Greek god. The Statue of Zeus was in the temple at Olympia in Greece. It was 40 feet tall. The statue's eyes were big jewels. Its hair, beard, and clothes were coated with real

gold. Phidia carved it from ivory about 435 BCE. At that time, he was the best artist in Greece. A fire ruined the statue about 462 CE.

Ptolemy Philadelphus built the Lighthouse of Pharos in 200 BCE. It stood on the island of Pharos near Alexandria. It guided ships into the harbor. Made of marble, it stood 407 feet tall. At all times, a fire burned at the top. Mirrors behind the fire made the light brighter. Sea captains could see it from far away. An earthquake wrecked it in 1375 CE. It was the tallest lighthouse ever built.

Check Your Understanding

1. Nebuchadnezzar ordered the building of the
   a. temple at Olympia.
   b. Statue of Zeus.
   c. Hanging Gardens of Babylon.
   d. Lighthouse of Pharos.

2. Which ancient structure was the most useful?
   a. the Great Pyramid at Giza
   b. the Statue of Zeus
   c. Hanging Gardens of Babylon
   d. the Lighthouse of Pharos

3. Were any of these ancient structures destroyed by fire?
   a. yes, the Statue of Zeus
   b. yes, the Lighthouse of Pharos
   c. yes, the Hanging Gardens of Babylon
   d. no

4. Who designed the Statue of Zeus?
   a. Nebuchadnezzar
   b. Ptolemy
   c. Phidia
   d. Philadelphus

/4

Warm-Up 23

Name _____

The Ice Ages

No one knows for sure what triggers an ice age. Most scientists think that about every 10,000 to 20,000 years, Earth wobbles a little bit. This causes a slight change to its orbit around the sun. As a result, the area near the North Pole gets less sunlight. Then the ice sheets that cover the Arctic Circle spread south. These ice sheets are called *glaciers*.

During an ice age, glaciers cover a lot of Earth's land. Where does this frozen water come from? It is water that has evaporated from the oceans. So the sea level drops all over the world. When the water level falls, land that had been underwater is revealed. Water absorbs the sun's heat better than land. This means that having less ocean water further cools Earth's atmosphere. In an ice age, a hot summer day would not be 88°F. It would be just 71°F. Only near the equator do temperatures remain stable.

We know that Earth has already had several ice ages. Each one lasted for thousands of years. The last ice age ended about 11,500 years ago. Many scientists agree that a new ice age could start at any time. However, global warming may counteract an ice age. This means that if an ice age began, global warming might cancel its effects.

Check Your Understanding

1. An ice age affects Earth about every
   a. 500 years.
   b. 1,000 years.
   c. 5,000 years.
   d. 10,000 years.

2. During an ice age, what happens second?
   a. Glaciers extent further south than usual.
   b. The North Pole gets less sunlight.
   c. The level of Earth's oceans falls.
   d. Earth's orbit changes slightly.

3. The area of Earth least affected by an ice age is near the
   a. equator.
   b. North Pole.
   c. South Pole.
   d. seacoasts.

4. What effect would global warming most likely have on glaciers?
   a. Glaciers might float to cooler places.
   b. More glaciers would form.
   c. Glaciers would form in Africa.
   d. Whole glaciers might melt.

/4

Warm-Up

24

Name _____

U.S. Anti-Slavery Laws

Congress passed laws in 1794 and 1807 to stop new slaves from coming into the United States. By 1815, the U.S. Navy had ships that patrolled Africa's west coast. They stopped ships heading toward the Americas. When a ship was found to be a slaver, it was seized. The slaver's crew was set free along with the captives. All were put ashore at Liberia. It is a nation on Africa's west coast. The slaver (ship) was taken to America and sold. The captain and officers stood trial in a U.S. Federal Court.

U.S. sailors hated working on these ships. The climate was hot and humid. They got tropical diseases. Many of the men were upset by the cruelty they saw on the slavers. When they did take over a slave ship, they had to nurse the captives back to health. This was a hard task, and many died. The sailors felt discouraged.

To get sailors to serve on these ships, the U.S. Navy gave prize money (in addition to regular pay) for each captured ship. It also paid $25 for each rescued slave. The money went to the ship's captain. He split it among the crew.

None of this helped the people who were already slaves in America. Their children were born into slavery, too. These were just the nation's first steps in acknowledging the evils of slavery.

Check Your Understanding

1. The anti-slavery laws of 1794 and 1807 helped
   a. kidnapped people on slave ships.
   b. the captains of slave ships.
   c. children born to slaves.
   d. people who owned slaves.

2. What happened to the crew working on the slave ship?
   a. They were sold into slavery.
   b. They were released in Liberia.
   c. They were executed for kidnapping.
   d. They stood trial in a U.S. Federal Court.

3. Many of the people living in Liberia are descendants of
   a. Egyptians.
   b. African royalty.
   c. freed slaves.
   d. the Japanese.

4. Which statement is false?
   a. The U.S. sailors earned extra pay based on how many slaves they rescued.
   b. Liberia is a nation on Africa's west coast.
   c. Captured slavers were sold in America.
   d. U.S. sailors were eager to work on the ships that searched for slavers.

/4

Warm-Up
25

Name _____

U.S. Presidents from Ohio

Would you like to be the U.S. president when you grow up? If so, you might want to move to Ohio or Virginia. Nearly one-third of all U.S. presidents have come from one of these states. Of the first 44 presidents, seven came from Ohio and seven came from Virginia.

Both Ohio and Virginia claim the man who had the shortest presidency. He had lived in both states at different times. His name is William Harrison. He gave the longest-ever inauguration speech. During it, he caught a cold. He died a month later.

James Garfield also came from Ohio. He had the second shortest presidency. A man shot him on July 2, 1881. Garfield died 10 weeks later. The killer had tried to get a government job. He had been turned down. He blamed Garfield.

William McKinley came from Ohio, too. He was president during the Spanish-American War. This war gave Cuba its freedom. It gave the United States the territories of Guam, Puerto Rico, and the Philippines. McKinley was re-elected. But then, in his second term, a man wrapped a bandage around his hand. He hid a gun under the cloth. When McKinley shook the man's hand, he shot him. McKinley died from the wound.

The other presidents from Ohio are Grant, Hayes, B. Harrison, Taft, and Harding.

Check Your Understanding

1. Which U.S. president served the shortest term?
   a. The article does not tell.
   b. William McKinley
   c. William Harrison
   d. James Garfield

2. At the end of the Spanish-American War, the United States took control of several territories, but not
   a. Cuba.
   b. Puerto Rico.
   c. Guam.
   d. the Philippines.

3. Who was the U.S. president during the Spanish-American War?
   a. Abraham Lincoln
   b. James Garfield
   c. William Harrison
   d. William McKinley

4. *Assassinated* means murdered for political reasons. Which U.S. president was *not* assassinated?
   a. James Garfield
   b. William Harrison
   c. Abraham Lincoln
   d. William McKinley

/4

Warm-Up

26 Flight Disappearances

Name _____

Amelia Earhart was the first woman to fly alone across the Atlantic Ocean. But a mystery surrounds her last flight. She and her navigator, Fred Noonan, vanished. No trace of them or their plane has ever been found. Many people have searched.

In May 1937, Amelia and Fred set out to fly around the world. She would be the first woman to do so. The U.S. Navy kept track of them. Things seemed fine. Then, on July 2, they radioed that they were low on gas. What happened next is unclear. People on several islands said that they saw a plane crash into the Pacific Ocean. Others said they saw the pair held as Japanese prisoners. Some think that the Japanese thought they were spies and killed them. We may never know.

In November 1971, a passenger said that he would blow up a jet as it flew over the state of Washington. D.B. Cooper made the pilot land the plane. In exchange for $200,000 cash and four parachutes, he let everyone get off. Just he and the pilot took off again. Cooper had no idea that the bills were marked with invisible ink. He jumped out the back door with the cash. He was never seen again. In 1980, a family went on a picnic. They found $5,800 of Cooper's marked bills. They were floating in the Columbia River.

Check Your Understanding

1. The main idea of this passage is that
    a. a mystery surrounds Amelia Earhart's last flight.
    b. D.B. Cooper was a hijacker.
    c. Amelia Earhart and Fred Noonan crashed into the Pacific Ocean.
    d. Amelia Earhart, Fred Noonan, and D.B. Cooper disappeared and were never found.

2. Based on her last radio call, Amelia most likely
    a. crash landed on an island and lost her memory.
    b. was killed for being a U.S. spy.
    c. ran out of gas and crashed into the ocean.
    d. landed on a deserted island and went into hiding.

3. In 1937, Amelia Earhart was unusual because she
    a. was a pilot.   c. was married.
    b. believed in women's rights.   d. left the United States to live in Japan.

4. Why did the police give marked bills to D.B. Cooper?
    a. Marked bills weigh more than unmarked ones, so Cooper had to drop the money or lose control of his parachute.
    b. They wanted to be able to track the money and find the hijacker.
    c. They hoped the plane would crash.
    d. They wanted the ink to get on the hijacker's hands and annoy him.

/4

Warm-Up 27

Name _____

Moving the U.S. Mail, 1753 to 1863

The U.S. Postal Service has changed a lot from its beginnings. In 1753, Benjamin Franklin set up the mail system in the colonies. He said that mail should be put in envelopes. That way it would be private. Before then, mail carriers could read anything they delivered! Early mail carriers rode horses. They earned three cents per mile in the summer. They made 3.5 cents per mile in the winter.

Early postmasters had small offices. They sorted the mail into cubbyholes. In 1789, Congress gave the federal government the sole power to offer mail service.

In 1813, all steamboats began carrying mail. All railroads became part of the mail system in 1838. Mailbags were hung from poles near the tracks. Conductors grabbed the bags as the train sped past! A town not on rail lines had its mail delivered to the nearest station. Then, it went the rest of the way in a horse-drawn wagon.

The person who got the mail paid the postage. This was true whether the person wanted the piece of mail or not! In 1855, Congress passed a law. All postage had to be prepaid. Five- and ten-cent stamps were printed.

Free home delivery service began for cities in 1863. Those who lived in a rural area had to rent a post office box.

Check Your Understanding

1. Who came up with the idea of putting mail into envelopes?
   a. the U.S. Postal Service
   b. Congress
   c. George Washington
   d. Ben Franklin

2. Which event occurred second?
   a. Congress gave the U.S. government the sole power to operate the mail service.
   b. Steamboats became mail routes and had to carry mail.
   c. All postage had to be prepaid by the sender.
   d. Railroads became mail routes and had to carry mail.

3. If you rent a post office box, it means that you
   a. get mail delivered to your house.
   b. can send all of your mail for free.
   c. go to the post office to pick up your mail.
   d. send all packages using U.S. mail and no other carrier.

4. In 1863, free home delivery of the U.S. mail was given to
   a. people living in cities.
   b. people living in rural areas.
   c. people living in the suburbs.
   d. every home in the nation.

/4

Name _____

Moving the U.S. Mail, 1902 to Now

Before 1902, people who lived on farms had to rent post office boxes. Then, the United States Postal Service started free rural delivery. The rural mail carriers earned just $50 a month. Out of that, they had to buy a horse, wagon, and sled. They had to pay for the horse's feed and care, too.

Just nine years later, the first airmail went between two towns in New York. Airmail pilots had a tough job. They could fly only during the day. They had no lights, radios, or maps. They followed railways. If they got lost, they flew low to read the railroad station signs. If the weather turned bad or they had engine trouble, they had to land in a field. Between 1918 and 1926, more than 30 airmail pilots died. In fact, the average survival for pilots was just 900 hours of flight. That's 23 weeks of work! By 1927, airline companies carried passengers. They started to take the U.S. mail. Now most mail goes by air.

By the 1960s, there was a lot of mail. To speed things up, 5-digit ZIP codes were added to all addresses. Today, people read and sort handwritten addresses. Optical Character Recognition (OCR) machines sort typed addresses. The OCR sprays lines on the bottom of the envelope. It can scan and spray 500 letters a minute.

Check Your Understanding

1. Today most mail travels by
   a. railroad.
   b. helicopter.
   c. airplane.
   d. truck.

2. ZIP codes were introduced in order to
   a. make it safer to be an airmail pilot.
   b. make it cost less to send a letter.
   c. slow down mail delivery.
   d. speed up mail delivery.

3. Why does the U.S. Postal Service use OCR machines?
   a. They print ZIP codes on envelopes and packages.
   b. They track where the mail comes from and where it goes.
   c. They can scan and sort letters rapidly.
   d. They can read handwritten addresses.

4. When was the first airmail flown?
   a. 1902
   b. 1911
   c. 1918
   d. 1927

/4

Warm-Up 29

Name _____

Native American Unsolved Mysteries

Of all the world's unsolved mysteries, those about Native Americans may be among the most interesting. Great civilizations rose. They built magnificent architecture. Then they vanished. We wonder how and why. But since the people left no written language, our questions may never be answered.

More than 800 years ago, the Anasazi lived in the Four Corners of the American Southwest. The land was dry. They grew crops through the use of ditches. They carved their homes into the cliffs. Some of these homes still exist. We call these people the Anasazi. But archaeologists do not know their real name. It is just one part of the mystery that occurred when

they vanished 600 years ago. No one knows what happened to them. Their villages show no signs of war, hunger, or disease.

Scattered across the American Midwest are mounds of varying sizes and shapes. The people built these mounds carrying baskets of dirt by hand. From the size and complexity of some of the earth mounds, they would have taken hundreds of years to make. One is the Great Serpent Mound in Ohio. It is a snake over 1,250 feet long. In a forest in Iowa, there are one bird and ten bear mounds. The shapes are only clear from an overhead view. No one knows the purpose of these mounds or why this culture disappeared.

Check Your Understanding

1. Great Serpent Mound is located
   a. near the Four Corners of the American Southwest.
   b. between two towns in Peru.
   c. in Ohio.
   d. in Iowa.

2. Why did the Native Americans create gigantic dirt mounds in the shapes of animals?
   a. They believed this would bring them good harvests.
   b. They believed this would help them to win wars.
   c. They believed this would protect the tribe from diseases.
   d. No one knows for sure.

3. Why might we never find the answers to these mysteries?
   a. There is no evidence left of Native American culture before the 1700s.
   b. Without written records we can only guess at what happened.
   c. Today's Native Americans believe they must keep these secrets sacred.
   d. Anyone who tries to find the answers mysteriously vanishes.

4. The Native Americans who built their homes into the cliffs had a tribal name. It is
   a. not definitely known.
   b. Anasazi.
   c. Nazca.
   d. Serpent.

/4

Warm-Up

30   Washington Irving, Author and Ghost

Name _____

Washington Irving's ghost is one of the best documented in history. Many witnesses swore that they saw him. It seems fitting that the man who wrote *The Legend of Sleepy Hollow* should turn into a ghost. It is one of America's most famous ghost stories.

Irving was one of the founders of the Astor Library in New York City. He spent many happy hours there before his death in 1859. Shortly after that, Dr. J. G. Cogswell was in the library at midnight. He heard a noise and went to see what made it. He saw a white-haired man sitting in a shadowy corner. The man was reading a book. Cogswell moved closer. He was shocked to see the man whose funeral he had just attended! Three nights later, Cogswell saw the **specter** again. The ghost did not seem aware of the doctor. Yet each time he got close, it quickly faded away. For years to come, people saw Irving in the Astor Library.

The man who wrote *Rip Van Winkle* and made "the headless horseman" a household term had said that he did not believe in ghosts. What must he have thought when he himself became one?

Check Your Understanding

1. Washington Irving wrote
   - a. *The Headless Horseman.*
   - b. *The Specter in the Astor Library.*
   - c. *Rip Van Winkle.*
   - d. Spanish ghost stories.

2. A synonym for **specter** is
   - a. monster.
   - b. ghost.
   - c. author.
   - d. librarian.

3. Washington Irving worked
   - a. as a doctor.
   - b. as a librarian.
   - c. as a funeral director.
   - d. to start a library.

4. From this passage you can tell that Washington Irving
   - a. wanted to be a stage actor.
   - b. wrote about the ghosts he saw during his life.
   - c. enjoyed reading and writing.
   - d. was best friends with Dr. J. G. Cogswell.

/4

Did You Know?

Warm-Up

1

Name _____

Sea Horses

What has a tail like a monkey, a head like a horse, and a pouch like a kangaroo? It's an odd fish called a sea horse. Sea horses have long, flexible tails that they use to cling to sea plants. They use their long snouts to suck up and eat plankton. Plankton are animals too tiny to see without a **microscope**.

Sea horses reproduce in an unusual way. The male has a pouch. The female lays up to 100 eggs in his pouch. The male carries the eggs around for six weeks. Then he labors to give birth to tiny, live babies. The babies hold each other's tails until they float to the safety of a patch of seaweed or a coral reef. Then they let go of each other and go their separate ways.

If they can avoid predators, the babies can live to be three years old. Because a sea horse must move through the water in an upright position, it cannot swim well. This means that it can't use speed to escape from predators. Many animals that try to eat a sea horse will spit it out. Why? Sea horses have bony knobs and spines covering their bodies. Sharks, sea turtles, barracudas, and stingrays still eat them anyway. So sea horses cling to coral reefs. They blend in by changing color to match their surroundings.

Check Your Understanding

1. Which event happens first?
   a. The sea horse babies float away.
   b. The female puts eggs into the male's pouch.
   c. The male gives birth to tiny babies.
   d. The male carries the eggs for weeks.

2. A **microscope** makes things appear
   a. brighter.
   b. darker.
   c. bigger.
   d. smaller.

3. Sea horses change color in order to
   a. hide from enemies.
   b. attract a mate.
   c. lure plankton closer.
   d. find a home.

4. A predator grabs a sea horse in its mouth. Instead of eating it, it spits it out because the
   a. sea horse bit the predator.
   b. predator wasn't really hungry.
   c. predator didn't like how the sea horse tasted.
   d. predator didn't like the sea horse's bony outer covering.

/4

Name _____

2   The Popular Product That Almost Wasn't

Sometimes popular products almost do not happen. Post-it® Notes is one example. When Spencer Silver worked for 3M Company, he made a weak glue. He showed it to Art Fry, another worker. They both agreed it was useless. Silver threw it out.

Then, in 1974, Art Fry wished he had a way to temporarily mark the pages in a book. He hated how bookmarks fell out. He recalled Silver's weak glue. The two men started to work on bookmarks made with the weak glue. It took them 18 months to get them right. They showed the product to the advertising managers at 3M. They didn't like it.

Fry thought about how he could use it in his daily life. He decided he'd like to put temporary notes in his office. He decided to make notepads. He took his new idea to the advertising department. They were doubtful. But they said they would give it a try.

The company made enough Post-it notepads to sell in four cities. It was a test to see if anyone liked them. Few people bought them. So 3M told the stores to give them away. Once people tried Post-it Notes, they liked them. Suddenly, people called the company, wanting to buy them! Today they are one of 3M's best-selling products.

Check Your Understanding

1. What is the main idea of the passage?
   a. If not for Art Fry's efforts, Post-it Notes would not have been invented.
   b. Post-it Notes are the most popular product in 3M history.
   c. Art Fry designed many new products for his employer, 3M.
   d. At first it was hard to get people to buy Post-it Notes.

2. What is another good title for this passage?
   a. "Giving Products Away Boosts Sales"
   b. "Successful 3M Products"
   c. "Making Bookmarks and Notepads"
   d. "The Sticky Story of Post-it Notes"

3. Why was it a clever idea to give away a product?
   a. It was a good way to get rid of stock.
   b. No one would have paid for the product anyway.
   c. People expect companies to give them gifts.
   d. Once people try a product, they often want to buy it.

4. You can conclude that the 3M managers
   a. decided to fire Art Fry.
   b. weren't pleased that they listened to Art Fry's idea.
   c. were glad they tried out Art Fry's idea.
   d. gave away a lot of products from then on.

/4

Warm-Up
3

Name _____

Not So Identical

Identical twins always come from the same egg. They look alike. They have the same DNA. Yet their fingerprints, handprints, and footprints will be different. Why? A person's prints come from his or her time in the mother's womb. Pressure on the growing child's hands, fingers, and feet help to create its prints. Each baby changes position. It touches itself. It touches its twin. It touches its mother's womb. The surface pressure on the skin forms the prints the child will have.

For a similar reason, the first cat ever cloned did not look like the original. It wasn't even close. The first cat was a calico. Its fur had black, white, and orange patches. Its DNA was put into a fertilized egg. This was put into a pregnant cat. When the cloned cat was born, its fur had the same colors, but its markings were very different.

An animal's coat markings are based on things that occur in the womb. Since conditions in the womb are never identical from one birth to another, no two animals will ever be identical. For example, the mother may get sick during one pregnancy. She may eat better during another. Her blood pressure or pulse may differ, too.

Check Your Understanding

1. Identical twins have the same
   a. DNA.
   b. handprints.
   c. footprints.
   d. fingerprints.

2. The first cloned cat
   a. came from the same egg as the original cat.
   b. had the same DNA as the original cat.
   c. looked exactly like the original cat.
   d. was a different color than the original cat.

3. A person's handprints form as a result of
   a. DNA.
   b. the length of the pregnancy.
   c. the mother's diet.
   d. surface pressure on the skin.

4. You can tell that a calico cat has
   a. colored patches on its fur.
   b. spotted fur.
   c. striped fur.
   d. solid-color fur.

/4

Warm-Up 4

Name _____

What You Didn't Know About George Washington

You know that George Washington was the first president of the United States. You might also know that he led the Continental Army during the American Revolution. But there are some things you may not know about George.

George was an Anglican. It is a type of Christian. But he believed in freedom of religion. He made it a point to go to many different Christian churches. He worshipped with the people in each one. He also showed support for Judaism. He wanted to act on his belief that each person's faith was valuable. His strong stance is one of the reasons we have freedom of religion.

The Continental Army spent one winter camped at Valley Forge. George gave his troops shots. These shots kept the men from getting smallpox. He built a hospital to take care of the sick, too. His wife worked for free as a nurse there. So did George. And he never took one cent in pay for leading the Continental Army!

When George's father died, George inherited his slaves. So, George owned slaves. But around 1775, he made a vow. He would never buy or sell a person. George did not let anyone mistreat his slaves. When he died, he had the 316 people set free.

Check Your Understanding

1. George Washington believed in
   a. winter camping as a fun pastime.
   b. trying to earn a lot of money.
   c. letting people practice their faith.
   d. buying and selling slaves.

2. If you were a soldier at Valley Forge and you got sick, you were
   a. not given any care.
   b. cared for in a hospital.
   c. given a pay raise.
   d. sent home.

3. If you were one of George Washington's slaves, you knew that you would
   a. have all your debts paid.
   b. be treated badly.
   c. not be sold.
   d. not get medical care.

4. Which statement about the Continental Army is false?
   a. George Washington made its men go to church.
   b. Martha Washington worked as nurse for it.
   c. One winter, it camped at Valley Forge.
   d. George Washington made sure that it was protected from smallpox.

/4

Warm-Up

Name _____

5 In-Line Skates

James Merlin made the first pair of in-line skates in 1760. His skates had wooden spools in a row. He wore them to a party and ran into a mirror. He never wore them again. Few people tried skating, and those that did copied Merlin's design. In 1863, James Plimpton decided to change the design. He made skates with four spread-out wheels. This style was the only kind of wheeled skate for over 100 years.

Chicago Roller Skate created an in-line roller skate in 1966. The product flopped. No one bought them. Then in 1980, Scott Olsen saw a pair. He played hockey and wanted to keep his skills strong year round.

He knew other hockey players and ice skaters wanted to train without ice, too. They needed skates that moved like ice skates. Olsen made a new pair of in-line skates. He called them Rollerblades.

People got excited when they saw the new skates. Even those who didn't ice skate wanted to try them. Once they did, they lost interest in roller skates. Now many people like in-line skating better than any other kind of skating.

Check Your Understanding

1. What is the main idea of the passage?
   a. In-line skates were popular during the 1700s.
   b. In-line skates have replaced roller skates in popularity.
   c. Hockey players and ice skaters are the only people who wear in-line skates.
   d. In-line skates did not become popular until more than 200 years after they were invented.

2. Who made the more recent design for in-line skates?
   a. James Merlin   c. James Plimpton
   b. Scott Olsen   d. Chicago Roller Skate

3. Why do you think James Merlin never wore his in-line skates after the party?
   a. He thought that they were too ugly.
   b. He never got invited to another party.
   c. He got hurt when he crashed into a mirror.
   d. He changed the design to have four spread-out wheels.

4. What professional athletes benefit the most from in-line skates?
   a. snowboarders   c. gymnasts
   b. basketball players   d. ice skaters

/4

Warm-Up 6

Mazes

Name _____

The first mazes were planted in the 1500s on the grounds of English and French palaces. Mazes were made for the enjoyment of royalty and royal guests. These mazes consisted of high hedges. It took years to grow them. First, yew or pine bushes were planted close together. Then, the bushes had to grow **dense** enough that no one inside the maze could peek through them. They had to grow tall enough so that no one could see over them, either.

One of the most famous mazes is at Hampton Court Palace in London. Just outside of the maze stands a tall chair. A person sitting in it can see over the whole maze. By shouting directions, he can guide anyone who is lost to an exit. The Pineapple Garden Maze is the world's largest hedge maze. It is on the Dole Plantation in Hawaii. The paths that wind through it are more than 2.5 miles long.

Corn mazes are popular today. It can take hours to find one's way out of one of these mazes. Tom Pearcy, a British farmer, enjoys making corn mazes. He has cut his cornfields into the shape of London's Big Ben clock and a Viking ship. In 2008, he made a corn maze in the shape of the Statue of Liberty. It was 12 times larger than the actual statue!

Check Your Understanding

1. The biggest hedge maze on Earth is in
    a. Great Britain.
    b. France.
    c. Hawaii.
    d. London.

2. The word **dense** means
    a. tall.
    b. wide.
    c. green.
    d. thick.

3. Why do people like mazes?
    a. They want to walk among fruit trees.
    b. They like to camp overnight in the center of the maze.
    c. They like the challenge of finding the way out.
    d. They like the feeling of always being lost.

4. Which statement is false?
    a. A person helps guide lost people in the Hampton Court Palace maze.
    b. Tom Pearcy designs corn mazes.
    c. The Statue of Liberty corn maze was ten times the size of the statue.
    d. Corn mazes have been cut in the shape of a clock and a ship.

/4

Name _____

Guide Dogs

Many blind people have guide dogs to help them get around. Yet nobody set out to train guide dogs; it happened by accident! Near the end of World War I, a German doctor went for a walk outside a hospital. He had his dog and a blind patient with him. Someone called the doctor back inside. When he returned, he found that his dog had led the blind man all the way across the hospital grounds.

The doctor wondered if a dog could be trained to lead a blind person. He started working with his dog, then other dogs, as well. His results were a success. In 1929, an American reporter wrote about the German's guide dog program. This led to the creation of the first American guide dog school.

German shepherds and Labrador retrievers are the most common guide dogs. They learn the meaning of voice commands and hand gestures. At home they get things for their owners. Some can even open the refrigerator door and get a gallon of milk. They also learn when to disobey an order. Say a guide dog is told to lead the person across a street. The dog sees a speeding van. It will not let the person step into the road. A guide dog must learn to make decisions—such as what to do when the sidewalk is blocked.

Check Your Understanding

1. Another good title for this passage is
   a. "Being Blind."
   b. "Guide Dogs Help the Blind."
   c. "First American Guide Dog School."
   d. "A Startling Discovery."

2. You can conclude that
   a. any dog can be a good guide dog.
   b. guide dogs don't live long lives.
   c. it takes a long time to train a guide dog.
   d. guide dogs are not very smart.

3. Why are guide dogs large breeds?
   a. Small dogs aren't as smart.
   b. The dogs need to be able to reach and carry things.
   c. Strangers would be more apt to pet a small dog.
   d. Big dogs cost less than little dogs.

4. Which is an example of a time when a guide dog would definitely have to make new decisions?
   a. when it takes its owner to a doctor's appointment
   b. when it must open the refrigerator door
   c. when it must lead its owner through the grocery store
   d. when it must lead its owner out of a burning building

/4

Warm-Up

8

Name _____

Frozen Animals Stay Alive

In places with cold winters, frogs hibernate. They burrow under the mud. They do not eat or move. They sleep and breathe slowly. When the mud warms up in spring, they wake up. However, if they freeze, they will not wake up.

The Canadian wood frog is different because its body can freeze and thaw without injury! Its body has adapted to live through very cold winters. When the temperature drops, the Canadian wood frog sits very still. Next, the frog's liver pumps out glucose. It keeps the water inside the frog from turning solid. Instead the water within the frog becomes thick like syrup.

The frog's skin does freeze, but it is not harmed. This is very rare. Almost no animal with a spine can survive such freezing. Scientists are studying this frog to learn how it freezes and thaws without damage.

Canadian wood frogs aren't the only animals that can freeze and thaw to new life. During the winter, earthworms continue to live and move around in the dirt below its frozen level. However, if a worm gets trapped in frozen soil, it freezes. Then it comes back to life when the ground thaws in the spring.

Check Your Understanding

1. All frogs that live in places with cold winters
   a. must move to warmer places to spend the winter.
   b. die in the fall.
   c. must hibernate.
   d. freeze and then thaw in the spring.

2. The glucose in the Canadian wood frog lets the water inside the frog
   a. thicken without freezing.
   b. freeze solid.
   c. warm up.
   d. leave its body.

3. Why do frogs hibernate?
   a. to grow larger
   b. to avoid harsh weather
   c. to reproduce
   d. to find a mate

4. Which statement is false?
   a. Glucose comes from the frog's liver.
   b. A Canadian wood frog can survive being frozen.
   c. Hibernating frogs do not move or eat for months.
   d. If an earthworm freezes under the dirt, it will die.

/4

Warm-Up 9

Name _____

Binti Jua and Jambo to the Rescue

Binti Jua is a gorilla. She was born in the Columbus Zoo in 1988. When she was three years old, she went to the Brookfield Zoo in Chicago. There, she became famous in 1996. She rescued a human child who fell into her enclosure.

When his parents weren't looking, a 3-year-old boy climbed the wall around the gorilla **enclosure**. He fell 18 feet onto concrete. He lay there, not moving. People watched, helpless, as Binti rushed over to him. Some feared that she would harm him. Although she was born and raised in a zoo, she was still a wild animal. A larger female gorilla approached, too. Binti growled at her. Next, Binti picked up the boy. She held him with her right arm.

This is how she often held her own infant. She carried the boy to the door where the zoo personnel appeared each day with food. Zoo staff took the boy from there. During the whole thing, her own 17-month-old baby clutched her back. The little boy was unconscious. He spent four days in a hospital. Thankfully, he recovered.

In a similar incident, a male gorilla named Jambo protected a 5-year-old boy who fell into his enclosure in 1986. Jambo kept the other gorillas away. He stroked the boy gently. Two zoo workers went in and got him.

Check Your Understanding

1. The little boy whom Binti Jua helped
   a. awoke and started screaming.
   b. recovered right away.
   c. was stunned but not injured.
   d. spent time in a hospital.

2. In these zoos, an **enclosure** is a(n)
   a. cage with metal bars.
   b. rescue method.
   c. area surrounded by a fence or wall.
   d. window.

3. Which event occurred last in real time?
   a. Two zoo workers went in and got the 5-year-old boy.
   b. Binti Jua carried a 3-year-old boy to a zoo worker.
   c. Jambo kept other gorillas away from the boy.
   d. Binti Jua kept other gorillas away from the boy.

4. You can conclude that both gorillas
   a. thought zoo workers would take care of the boys.
   b. dislike humans.
   c. thought the boys were baby gorillas.
   d. were afraid that the boys might hurt their own infants.

/4

Warm-Up 10

Name _____

The U.S. Supreme Court

How does the U.S. Supreme Court work? It is different from all other courts in America. Its job is to test each case against the Constitution. First, the nine judges must want to hear the case. Each term, hundreds of cases are submitted. Just two dozen are heard. If the Supreme Court refuses to hear a case, the lower court's decision is **affirmed**.

Once the Court decides to hear a case, the lawyer for each side has 30 minutes to speak before the judges. There are no witnesses. No one can interrupt—except for the judges. They can ask questions. A red light warns the lawyer that five minutes remain. A white light means that the lawyer must stop speaking.

After hearing both sides, the judges go into a room. They talk about the case. They are alone, and no recording of any kind is made. At last the judges come to a decision. Not all of them must agree—just the majority. Then, a member of the majority writes the Court's opinion (decision). It takes about a month. Why? All of the majority judges must agree. That causes plenty of rewrites. Any judge can write his or her own opinion to say why he or she does not agree with the decision. The Supreme Court's opinion is binding on all other U.S. courts.

Check Your Understanding

1. Who presents a case to the U.S. Supreme Court?
   a. two lawyers and a panel of witnesses
   b. two lawyers and a judge from a lower court
   c. two lawyers
   d. a panel of witnesses

2. On the U.S. Supreme Court, a minority justice is one who
   a. makes a ruling that binds all other courts in the United States.
   b. causes the most rewrites in the Court's opinion.
   c. writes the Court's opinion.
   d. does not agree with the majority ruling.

3. About how many cases does the U.S. Supreme Court hear each term?
   a. 9   c. 24
   b. 12   d. hundreds

4. The word **affirmed** means
   a. agreed with.   c. changed.
   b. reduced.   d. overruled.

/4

Warm-Up

Name _____

11   The World's Most Dangerous Animals

The last bad dream you had about an animal attack might have starred a big cat, shark, or wolf. But those animals, while scary, kill few people. The most dangerous animals on Earth will surprise you. They are ranked based on how deadly they are to humans.

The mosquito is public enemy number one. Mosquitoes have killed more people than any other animal. How? They spread three deadly diseases: malaria, yellow fever, and dengue fever. Each year, these diseases kill millions of people. Mosquitoes are a huge threat in Africa.

The cone shell looks like a big snail. If a person picks it up, it shoots a poison harpoon. The harpoon comes from the end of its shell. Within seconds, the person will die. The sea wasp is also called the box jellyfish. Its tentacles are 16 feet in length. It wraps them around a swimmer and stings. The person will die in a few hours. Even if this jellyfish is dead on the beach, it can still sting!

The spitting cobra is a nasty snake in India. It is poisonous. It lives to bite! It kills over 50,000 people each year. Africa has poisonous snakes, too. Yet the elephant kills more than 600 Africans each year. And hippos kill 200 more.

Striped sea snakes live in the Indian Ocean. Although their bites do not hurt at all, they are deadly.

Check Your Understanding

1. Which animal kills the most people each year?
   a. the spitting cobra   c. the cone shell
   b. the mosquito   d. the sea wasp

2. Which dangerous animal lives in saltwater?
   a. the hippo   c. the striped sea snake
   b. the spitting cobra   d. the mosquito

3. If you live in Africa, you don't need to fear
   a. elephants.   c. mosquitoes.
   b. hippos.   d. spitting cobras.

4. Why are big cats and wolves less deadly to humans than the animals described in the passage?
   a. Wolves and big cats try to avoid people.
   b. Wolves and big cats never encounter people.
   c. Wolves and big cats have mild venom.
   d. Wolves and big cats enjoy being with people and don't want to hurt them.

/4

Warm-Up

12

Name _____

Rice Feeds the World

Did you know that 70 percent of Earth's human population eats rice as a staple? A staple is a main food source. In America, bread is a staple. Rice grows in flooded fields called *paddies*. It grows especially well in warm, tropical places where the people can harvest two crops each year. Rice keeps for a long time. It does not need refrigeration. Rice is healthy and easy to digest. That's why one of the first solid foods you feed a baby is rice cereal.

Rice was first grown in Asia. Traders spread it around. Yet it came to the Americas by accident! In 1694, a ship loaded with rice left Madagascar (off the shore of Africa). It sailed around the Cape of Good Hope at the base of Africa. Then it headed toward Europe. However, it sailed into a hurricane. The storm's strong winds blew the ship across the Atlantic Ocean.

The ship ran aground off what is now the South Carolina coast. The settlers there helped the crew to fix the ship. The captain paid them with rice. The settlers planted the seeds and were happy with the crop. They had so much rice that they could trade the extra. Rice's "fame" spread across America. Now rice grows on every continent except Antarctica.

Check Your Understanding

1. Which statement is *not* true?
   a. Traders spread rice from Asia to Africa.
   b. Babies eat rice cereal.
   c. Asians settlers first brought rice to North America.
   d. Rice keeps a long time without refrigeration.

2. A rice paddie is a
   a. flooded field planted with rice.
   b. kind of pancake made with rice.
   c. dessert pudding made with rice.
   d. stalk of rice that is not eaten.

3. Rice was first grown in North America during the
   a. 1600s.
   b. 1700s.
   c. 1800s.
   d. 1900s.

4. Rice is a main food source for
   a. 1 out of every 70 people.
   b. 10 out of every 70 people.
   c. 50 out of every 70 people.
   d. 70 out of every 100 people.

/4

Warm-Up

13 Bamboo

Name _____

If you've heard of bamboo, it was probably as food for panda bears. Get ready to hear a lot more about bamboo. It is taking the world by storm.

Bamboo is the fastest growing known plant. Although it is a grass, its hollow stem looks like a tree trunk. People have discovered that bamboo has many uses. In Asia, whole houses are made of bamboo lumber. In China, some companies make paper using bamboo. This plant even makes music—it is used in flutes around the world.

In the United States, people use bamboo for flooring and kitchen countertops. It is 10 percent harder than maple, yet grows tall enough to harvest in just four years. It would take a maple tree 60 years to grow to the same height.

The fastest-growing use for bamboo is as a fabric. The cloth has good properties. No one is allergic to it. That makes it ideal for those with sensitive skin. It keeps the body cool in summer and warm in winter. Bamboo clothing feels as soft as silk or cashmere. But it does not require dry cleaning as those fabrics do. The cloth also drapes like silk without wrinkling.

Check Your Understanding

1. Bamboo is not used to make
   a. paper.
   b. fabric.
   c. lumber.
   d. soap.

2. You can tell that silk
   a. must be dry cleaned.
   b. is expensive.
   c. does not wrinkle.
   d. is not at all like bamboo fabric.

3. Why is it better to use bamboo flooring than maple flooring?
   a. Bamboo grows back slower.
   b. Bamboo resists nicks and dents.
   c. Bamboo will not stain.
   d. Bamboo costs more.

4. Complete this analogy: *bamboo* is to *grass* as *maple* is to
   a. *building.*
   b. *lumber.*
   c. *tree.*
   d. *flooring.*

/4

Warm-Up

14   Yawning *is* Contagious

Name _____

Have you ever noticed that when someone else yawns, within a few minutes you feel the urge to yawn, too? Yawning is a reflex. But most of our reflexes—such as dropping something that's too hot—have nothing to do with other people. So why is it that if you yawn, I'll want to yawn, too?

Many animals yawn when they are tired. But humans and chimps are the only ones who yawn because someone else already did. This means yawning is not a pure reflex like blinking is. You blink to protect your eye or to bathe it in tears to keep it clean. You must concentrate to force your eyes not to blink. And eventually your body will make you blink.

It will not force you to yawn. Instead, scientists think that yawning is a social behavior.

Long ago, cave people yawned to show the other members of their group that they felt tired. When one person yawned and then others did, too, the tribe's leader may have known that it was time to take a rest. Yawning kept everyone together and safe.

Here's more proof for the social theory: Human babies can yawn at birth. But they only yawn in response to others' yawns after they reach the age of two. That is when babies first react to how another person feels.

Check Your Understanding

1. Before the age of two, when a human yawns, it means that the baby
   a. is tired.
   b. wants to be held.
   c. is responding to another person's feelings.
   d. is hungry.

2. Why do human toddlers yawn after someone else yawns?
   a. They are always tired.
   b. They have learned to respond to other people's signals.
   c. They want to please the person who yawned.
   d. They want their diapers changed.

3. In cave people, yawning let the tribe leader know that
   a. it was time for the group to take a rest.
   b. there was danger close by.
   c. the group was low on oxygen.
   d. the group needed to find more food.

4. Which of the following is *not* one of your reflexes?
   a. gagging when something touches the back of your throat
   b. closing your eyes when something is thrown at your face
   c. sneezing
   d. laughing

/4

Warm-Up

15

Name _____

The Story of Jeep

Did you know that the company that created the jeep went out of business because two other companies got to build them? It sounds crazy. But it happened.

American Bantam Car Company designed the jeep. It had four-wheel drive. This let it go almost anywhere. For a long time, Bantam tried to get the U.S. Army to buy jeeps. At last, in July 1940, the Army ordered 70 jeeps. They were tested and found to be useful.

The Japanese attacked Pearl Harbor in December 1941. The United States entered into World War II. The Army told Bantam it was too small. It could not make enough jeeps quickly. So Bantam got a contract to make just 2,675 jeeps. The Army gave the jeep plans to two bigger carmakers. Ford and Willys-Overland shared a contract to make 640,000 jeeps!

Bantam went bankrupt. The war ended. Hundreds of jeeps were left in the Philippines. Clever Filipinos **modified** them. They added seats for passengers and metal roofs for shade. They painted their "jeepneys" bright colors. These were the first buses in the war-torn nation.

After the war, Willys-Overland changed the jeep. It turned it into a family car. It was made into the first station wagon. (It was the ancestor of today's minivan.) Today Chrysler owns the brand name Jeep.

Check Your Understanding

1. Which organization designed the jeep?
   a. the U.S. Army
   b. Ford
   c. Willys-Overland
   d. American Bantam Car Company

2. A synonym for **modified** is
   a. sold.
   b. changed.
   c. scrapped.
   d. built.

3. A jeepney is
   a. a jeep that has been made into a bus.
   b. an old jeep that's been fixed up and shown in an auto show.
   c. a new style of jeep made for the 21st century.
   d. the name of the first station wagon.

4. Why was the contract for the majority of jeeps *not* given to its designer?
   a. Other companies had better jeep designs.
   b. The company refused to make them.
   c. Other companies could make jeeps for less money.
   d. The company wasn't large enough to make lots of jeeps fast.

/4

Warm-Up

16   **World's Largest Ice Sculptures: Icebergs**

Name _____

When you hear the word *iceberg*, you think of something big and white. But did you know that icebergs can be striped? If a crack in the ice fills with water that freezes fast, no bubbles form. That frozen water forms a blue stripe. And, if part of a moving glacier breaks off as an iceberg, it may have black, yellow, or brown stripes. These stripes are layers of dirt. The glacier scraped them off the land.

A huge iceberg broke off Antarctica in 1987. It held so much fresh water that it could have given every person on Earth half a gallon of water per day for 330 years! Another big iceberg was called B-15. It broke off Antarctica in 2000. It was twice the size of Delaware! It took five years to totally break up.

Icebergs have a bad reputation. They got it when the *Titanic* sank after hitting one in 1912. More than 1,500 of those aboard lost their lives. Striking an iceberg can still sink a ship. So now there is an air ice patrol. It warns ships about icebergs.

Icebergs aren't always bad. In 1875, the *Caledonia* wrecked off the coast of Canada. The ship went down so fast that the men couldn't launch the lifeboats. Yet the crew of 82 survived. They sat on an iceberg until help arrived.

Check Your Understanding

1. Icebergs do *not* have stripes that are
   a. blue.
   b. brown.
   c. purple
   d. black.

2. The iceberg B-15
   a. broke off Antarctica in 1987.
   b. was twice as big as Delaware.
   c. was gone in four years.
   d. caused the *Titanic* to sink.

3. Which ship's crew was saved by an iceberg?
   a. the *Canada*
   b. the *Antarctica*
   c. the *Titanic*
   d. the *Caledonia*

4. Why are ships in less danger from icebergs today than in the past?
   a. An air ice patrol warns ships about icebergs in the area.
   b. Modern ships can ram icebergs without getting damaged.
   c. Ships are no longer at sea at the same time as icebergs.
   d. Global warming has reduced the number of icebergs floating in the ocean.

/4

Warm-Up
17

Name _____

Storms that Caused Discoveries

You know that Columbus "sailed the ocean blue" in 1492. He was looking for India but found the New World. But did you know that some discoveries were made when the ship's captain wasn't looking for land? These discoveries were the results of storms at sea.

Long ago, the only way to get around was by sail power. The wind blew and moved the ship. Sometimes the wind blew the ship places that the captain did not intend to go. That's how the first European reached Greenland. Gunnbjorn was a Viking. In 930, his ship was blown there during a storm. In 1488, Bartolomeu Dias, a Portuguese captain, was sailing in the Atlantic Ocean. A storm pushed his ship all the way to the southern tip of Africa. As a result, he was the first European to sail around the Cape of Good Hope.

The first Europeans to set foot in Japan were shipwrecked. In 1543, they were on a Chinese ship. It went down in a storm off the coast of Japan. The men were saved. They later went back to Europe. They told others about the island nation.

In 1616, Dirk Hartog got lost sailing near the Philippines. He saw a big storm brewing. He wanted to reach land—any land. The Dutchman was the first European to land in Australia.

Check Your Understanding

1. The man who discovered Greenland was
   a. Japanese.
   b. Portuguese.
   c. Dutch.
   d. a Viking.

2. Which event occurred third?
   a. Bartolomeu Dias sailed around the Cape of Good Hope.
   b. Christopher Columbus discovered the New World.
   c. Gunnbjorn's ship was blown to Greenland.
   d. The first Europeans visited Japan.

3. Which statement is true?
   a. Europeans visited Japan before Greenland.
   b. A sea captain looking for Australia discovered the Philippines.
   c. Europeans knew about North America before they knew about Australia.
   d. A Dutch sea captain was the first to sail around the Cape of Good Hope.

4. Why did Captain Hartog want to reach land?
   a. He knew that being at sea during a violent storm was dangerous.
   b. He wanted to convert the natives to Christianity.
   c. He wanted to be the first European to set foot in Australia.
   d. His ship was sinking near the Philippines.

/4

Warm-Up 18

Name _____

The Sweet Story of Jelly Beans

When Ronald Reagan was president, there was a bowl of them in nearly every room of the White House. The fictional character Harry Potter made them famous. He ate Bertie Bott's Every Flavor Beans. They came in crazy flavors like rotten eggs and dog food. What are they? Jelly beans!

Around 1900, jelly beans first appeared in candy stores. All the colors were separate. You bought them one at a time. They cost a penny apiece. They were popular. Soon they were sold by the pound.

In the 1930s, many people were poor. Candy sales were down. Then, an ad in newspapers told children that the Easter Bunny would bring them jelly beans. Easter always happens in spring.

The jelly bean shape is similar to an egg shape. Eggs **symbolize** birth. Many birds are born in spring. Parents bought the jelly beans to put in their children's Easter baskets. A tradition was born.

In the mid 1970s, the Jelly Belly Company (called the Herman Goelitz Candy Company back then) changed jelly beans. The company started to make unusual flavors like watermelon and tangerine. Now there are nearly 100 flavors. People love jelly beans. In fact, people ate 16 billion last year. If you lined that many up end to end, they would circle Earth three times!

Check Your Understanding

1. When jelly beans were first sold, how many could you get for a dime?
   a. 5
   b. 10
   c. 20
   d. 30

2. A synonym for **symbolize** is
   a. represent.
   b. help.
   c. deny.
   d. resist.

3. Why are jelly beans connected to Easter?
   a. Easter is in the spring, and bunnies hatch from eggs.
   b. Jelly beans taste like eggs, which are a sign of Easter.
   c. Easter is in the spring, and birds' eggs hatch then.
   d. Jelly beans cost less than chocolate Easter bunnies.

4. Which event occurred last?
   a. Jelly beans were sold one at a time.
   b. Jelly beans were sold by the pound.
   c. Candy makers ran ads promising children jelly beans in their Easter baskets.
   d. Jelly beans came in dozens of different flavors.

/4

Name _____

Pelorus Jack

Near the New Zealand coast, a dolphin popped up beside a ship's bow in 1888. He appeared at the start of the French Pass. It was foggy, so the *Brindle's* captain followed the animal through the swift currents and sharp underwater rocks. The ship reached its dock safely.

Wise sailors feared the French Pass. This narrow strip of fast-flowing water had claimed dozens of ships and hundreds of lives. From that day on, Pelorus Jack the dolphin escorted each ship that entered the French Pass. No ship that followed him ever wrecked.

In 1903, a passenger on the *Penguin* shot Pelorus Jack. Luckily, the dolphin was just hurt. He disappeared for two weeks.

Then, he suddenly appeared once more to guide ships. He helped each ship through the French Pass except for one: the *Penguin*. How he recognized that ship is anyone's guess. He never helped it again. No one was surprised when the *Penguin* wrecked in the French Pass.

In 1912, Pelorus Jack vanished just as mysteriously as he appeared. He probably died of old age. Dolphins only live about 35 years. He had been "on the job" for nearly a quarter of a century.

Check Your Understanding

1. The French Pass is a
  a. waterway.
  b. ship.
  c. sailing maneuver.
  d. kind of dolphin.

2. Which event happened third?
  a. Pelorus Jack helped the *Brindle*.
  b. The dolphin vanished for two weeks.
  c. Pelorus Jack had a bad experience with the *Penguin*.
  d. The *Penguin* sank.

3. The dolphin refused to guide the *Penguin* after 1903. Why?
  a. The ship had struck and injured Pelorus Jack's mate.
  b. Pelorus Jack knew the ship was destined to be wrecked.
  c. Pelorus Jack knew that someone aboard that ship had shot him.
  d. Pelorus Jack knew the captain hunted and killed dolphins.

4. During his life, Pelorus Jack was most famous in
  a. New Zealand.
  b. France.
  c. the United States.
  d. Antarctica.

/4

Warm-Up 20

Name _____

The Gulf Stream

Have you ever heard of the Gulf Stream? It is a long, powerful ocean current. Its water flows along the coasts of North America and Europe. It is a wide river of warm water. It starts near the equator and heads north. It follows the East Coast of the United States. Near Cape Cod, Massachusetts, the current turns to the right. It crosses the ocean and then splits.

Some of the water goes south past Spain and Africa. The rest flows along the coast of Great Britain and Ireland. The Gulf Stream's warm water heats the air above it. That is why parts of Ireland are so warm that palm trees grow! And Great Britain has milder winters than Newfoundland, Canada. Yet both places are the same distance north of the equator.

About 500 years ago, ship captains discovered the Gulf Stream. They used it to make their ocean **voyages** shorter. They could cover 75 more miles per day if they sailed from America to Europe using the current. But if they sailed against the current on the trip from Europe to America, they could be slowed down so much that they would arrive two weeks late!

Check Your Understanding

1. What happens first?
   a. The Gulf Stream flows across the ocean.
   b. The Gulf Stream flows north from the equator.
   c. The Gulf Stream splits with some water flowing north and the rest going south.
   d. The Gulf Stream goes along the East Coast of the United States.

2. Another word for **voyages** is
   a. waves.
   b. adventures.
   c. journeys.
   d. problems.

3. Why did a ship's captain need to know about the Gulf Stream?
   a. so he could always avoid it
   b. so he wouldn't get shipwrecked
   c. so he could avoid dangerous currents
   d. so he could use it to travel faster

4. If the Gulf Stream changed where it flowed, how would Earth be affected?
   a. It would cause severe thunderstorms.
   b. The climate would change in several places.
   c. There would be huge undersea earthquakes.
   d. There would be big volcanic eruptions.

/4

Warm-Up 21

Name _____

Snowboarding

No one is sure who started the sport of snowboarding. Some say it was Jack Burchett. In 1929, he tied his feet to a piece of plywood. He held onto a piece of rope attached to the front of the board. Then he rode down a snowy hill. In the 1950s, some surfers and skateboarders also had homemade boards.

The first **manufactured** snowboard came out in 1965. The Snurfer looked like a plywood skateboard without wheels. The rider put his feet in tracks formed by steel tacks. A rope attached to the board's front let the rider hold on. However, these boards were banned at ski resorts. So the sport didn't really take off.

Yet people didn't give up. They used new designs and better materials that improved the boards. As the styles changed, snowboarding grew more popular. Today ski slopes worldwide welcome snowboards. The sport is growing in popularity. In fact, some predict it will overtake skiing by 2015.

Check Your Understanding

1. Thirty-three years after the Snurfer, snowboarding came to the Olympic Winter Games. In what year was it made an Olympic sport?
   a. 1998
   b. 1994
   c. 2002
   d. 2006

2. The word **manufactured** means
   a. acceptable.
   b. made in a factory.
   c. professional.
   d. used at a ski resort.

3. What does the passage mean when it says that snowboarding will overtake skiing?
   a. that skiing will go out of style for good
   b. that snowboarding will be less expensive than skiing
   c. that snowboarding will become more popular than skiing
   d. that snowboarding will be less popular than skiing

4. You can conclude that the brand name Snurfer comes from combining the words
   a. skateboard and skier.
   b. skateboard and snow.
   c. snowboard and skier.
   d. snow and surfer.

/4

Warm-Up

22 Dandelions: Weed, Flowers, or Food?

Name _____

Did you know that hundreds of years ago, no dandelions grew in North America? Then Europeans arrived. They had dandelion seeds on their clothes. The seeds fell from their clothes onto the ground. Since then, dandelions have spread all over the continent.

Most people view dandelions as weeds. They do not want them in their yards. Some people think that dandelion flowers are pretty. Others think that dandelions taste good. They cook dandelion leaves or put them into a fresh salad. The leaves must be picked before the flowers bloom, or they will taste bad. Some people make dandelion flowers into wine.

Dandelions lie dormant during the winter. When the spring comes, they bloom. Each night, their bright yellow flowers close up. When the sun shines the next day, they open up again.

Dandelion flowers are very unusual. They do not have to get pollen from another dandelion flower in order to form seeds. So after several days, the yellow flower turns white and puffy. A tiny brown seed forms at the bottom of each white petal. When the wind blows, the petals fly away. Each white petal acts like a parachute. It carries a seed. New dandelions grow where these seeds land.

Check Your Understanding

1. New dandelions
   a. can be far away from the parent dandelion.
   b. must grow near the parent dandelion.
   c. come up from the roots of a dandelion.
   d. are bigger than the parent dandelion.

2. Which event happens last in the life cycle of a dandelion?
   a. The dandelions grow yellow flowers.
   b. The seeds blow away.
   c. Seeds form at the base of the white petals.
   d. The petals turn white.

3. When is the best time to pick dandelion leaves to eat?
   a. before the flowers bloom   c. in the winter
   b. after the flowers bloom   d. after dark

4. Picture the first dandelion seeds coming to North America on a woman's clothing. What is she wearing?
   a. jeans and a T-shirt   c. a long dress
   b. a business suit   d. a pair of shorts and a tank top

/4

Warm-Up

23

Name _____

The Weight, the Wind, and the Wobbling

Bridges are amazing structures. They must stand up to huge stresses. First, they must carry a lot of weight. They must be able to have every bit of their length covered by cars and trucks. Some bridges even carry cars, trucks, and trains at the same time. Next, they must withstand strong winds. Depending on where they stand, bridges may have to face hurricanes. That means enduring 200-mile-per-hour blasts. A bridge in an earthquake zone must be able to bear strong shaking. There are two natural hazards that no one can design a bridge to withstand: tornadoes and volcanoes. Both disasters are sudden and violent.

Today, engineers design bridges on computers. Then they use computer models to test it. They need to see if the bridge can survive the weight, the wind, and the wobbling. They do all of this before they ever start to build the bridge.

The longest bridges are often suspension, which have their roadways hanging from cables. One of these is Japan's Akashi-Kaikyo Bridge. It has four lanes. It links a city to an island. It is nearly 2.5 miles long. It was designed to hold up even in a strong 8.5 scale earthquake and 177-mile-per-hour winds.

The world's tallest road bridge is another suspension one. It is in Colorado. The Royal Gorge Bridge carries traffic about 1,000 feet above the Arkansas River.

Check Your Understanding

1. All bridges must be
   a. able to carry great weight.
   b. very long.
   c. able to withstand earthquakes.
   d. suspension bridges.

2. The world's tallest road bridge is in
   a. Australia.
   b. Japan.
   c. Colorado.
   d. Arkansas.

3. The Akashi-Kaikyo Bridge stands in a place that may have
   a. floods.
   b. tornadoes and landslides.
   c. volcanic eruptions.
   d. hurricanes and earthquakes.

4. You can tell that Colorado's Royal Gorge is
   a. in an area that has floods.
   b. very deep.
   c. in an area that has earthquakes.
   d. 2.5 miles long.

/4

Warm-Up

24   Heinz 57 Varieties

Name _____

Do you like ketchup? Then you'll like the story of H. J. Heinz. He started the Heinz Company to sell his mother's horseradish. The year was 1869. Soon he decided to make ketchup, too.

Back then, even the **condiments** for a meal were made from scratch! Heinz knew that women didn't want to make every item for every meal. Yet most people were scared of prepared products. They knew they could get botulism, a fatal disease, from improperly canned goods. So, Heinz used advertising in a way that no one had before. He ran ads in newspapers and magazines. These ads guaranteed that his canned goods were pure. In 1906, the U.S. government set standards for canned goods with the Pure Food and Drug Act. By then, Heinz already owned the ketchup market. Heinz sold more ketchup than any other company in the world. That remains true today.

Heinz was ahead of his time. He was the first to give away samples of his product in stores. He ran his assembly lines 24 hours a day during the harvest season. This let fresh tomatoes be processed fast. He coined the name *Heinz 57 Varieties* because he liked how it sounded. (He didn't want to be limited to a certain number of products.) Heinz lived his motto, "Do a common thing uncommonly well."

Check Your Understanding

1. Heinz started his company in order to sell
   a. ketchup.
   b. horseradish.
   c. pickles.
   d. relish.

2. Which is a **condiment**?
   a. beef
   b. butter
   c. sugar
   d. ketchup

3. Heinz was the first company to
   a. give away samples.
   b. run advertisements.
   c. make ketchup.
   d. know about botulism.

4. How did Heinz get people to buy his canned products?
   a. He coined the name *Heinz 57 Varieties*.
   b. He helped people who got botulism.
   c. He advertised that they were safe to eat.
   d. He ran his assembly lines day and night during harvest time.

/4

Warm-Up 25

Name _____

Wacky Waterspouts

Would you believe that one day in France it rained frogs? It happened in a small town near Paris. It started out just a typical rainy day. People went out with raincoats and umbrellas. Suddenly thousands of frogs fell from the sky. They smashed through car windows. They bounced off people's heads. What happened?

Scientists believe a waterspout made the frogs fall. Waterspouts are tornadoes that form over large lakes or oceans. A waterspout forms when warm, moist air meets cold, dry air. This creates a spinning cloud. Just like a land tornado, a waterspout lifts things up and spins them around. Then it drops them far away— sometimes up to 100 miles away!

A waterspout lasts longer than a tornado. But it loses power when it crosses land. As its strength **diminishes**, the things it sucked up from the water fall to the ground.

There have been a few waterspouts reported in America. Snails fell in Pennsylvania in 1869. Seven years later hundreds of snakes fell in Tennessee. In Louisiana, thousands of fish rained down in 1949.

Check Your Understanding

1. Snakes fell from the sky in
   a. Louisiana.
   b. Pennsylvania.
   c. Tennessee.
   d. Florida.

2. An antonym for **diminishes** is
   a. changes.
   b. fades.
   c. decreases.
   d. increases.

3. In the formation of a waterspout, what would happen third?
   a. Water animals are sucked up out of the water.
   b. Warm air and cold air meet over water.
   c. A spinning funnel cloud forms.
   d. Animals fall from the sky.

4. How do tornadoes and waterspouts differ?
   a. The winds in waterspouts spin faster than those in tornadoes.
   b. Waterspouts can't move over land; tornadoes can.
   c. Tornadoes cause less damage than waterspouts.
   d. Tornadoes don't form over water; waterspouts do.

/4

Warm-Up 26

Name _____

Unique Languages

When people talk, they borrow words from each other. French, Spanish, and Italian are similar. If people know one of these languages, they often can figure out what's being said in one of the others. The English language uses many words from other languages. Examples include *kindergarten* (German), *canyon* (Spanish), and *balcony* (Italian).

Some societies developed cut off from other people. In these cases, their languages will be unique. The Pirahã tribe lives in the Amazon rain forest. They are not near any other people. They have a language that few outside the tribe can understand. The people use just one kind of syllable. They do not have tenses.

Their language has no written form.

The Maya live in Mexico. They have one of the purest languages in the world. Hundreds of years ago, the Spanish took over their land. They made the people speak Spanish. The Maya learned Spanish. But they taught their children the Mayan language, too. Now, even though everyone around them speaks Spanish, they still use their language. The only Spanish words they use are ones for which there is no Mayan word. So, they use the Spanish word for "horse." Why? The Spanish brought horses to the New World in 1519.

Check Your Understanding

1. Where does the Pirahã tribe live?
   a. in Spain
   b. in France
   c. in the Amazon rain forest
   d. in Mexico

2. Which language would probably be the hardest one for an outsider to learn?
   a. Italian
   b. Pirahãn
   c. French
   d. Mayan

3. Before the Spanish came to Mexico, the Maya
   a. had never seen a horse.
   b. had no language.
   c. used words from other languages.
   d. wanted to meet the Pirahã.

4. Why are the French, Spanish, and Italian languages so similar?
   a. The people wanted to make their languages easy to learn.
   b. The people wanted their children to know all three languages.
   c. The languages are all based on English.
   d. The nations where these languages started are close to each other in Europe.

/4

Name _____

Naming the States

Have you ever wondered how the 50 states were named? Some have the same names that the Native Americans gave to the area. They used descriptions to name places. Missouri means "river of the big canoes." Michigan means "great water." Ohio is "great river." Massachusetts means "people who live near the great hill." Connecticut means "beside the long tidal river." Hawaii is the word for "homeland."

Other states' names come from the English language. Indiana stands for "land of Indians." The English King George II named Georgia after himself. Both North and South Carolina were named for the English King Charles I. Maine is short for "mainland." New Hampshire was named for a settler's home in England. Each state that begins with "New" was named after another place.

The Spanish named some of the states. In the Spanish language, Florida means "feast of flowers." Montana means "mountain." Nevada means "snowcapped." The French King Louis XIV owned Louisiana. He named the area after himself. Later he sold it to the United States.

The reasons behind some names aren't clear. Rhode Island was named for a Greek island. Texas comes from a Caddo Native American word that means "friends." California was a made-up name in a book.

Check Your Understanding

1. What is the main idea of this passage?
   a. States' names come from a variety of sources.
   b. The reasons behind most states' names are unclear.
   c. Native Americans named nearly every state.
   d. You can see the English influence in most of the states' names.

2. You can guess that the state of Washington was named after
   a. a Native American tribe.   c. an English king.
   b. the first U.S. president.   d. a Spanish word.

3. Which state's name comes from the Spanish language?
   a. Nevada   c. California
   b. Ohio   d. Texas

4. Which state name honors a king?
   a. Maine   c. Michigan
   b. Montana   d. Louisiana

/4

Warm-Up

28

Name _____

Mysteries in Peru

Peru is a nation in South America. It has two mysteries that archaeologists want to solve. One is a set of spectacular **geoglyphs**. They lie between the towns of Nazca and Palpa. These lines form drawings that stretch for 50 miles across the plateau. These huge pictures and thousands of perfectly straight lines have been preserved for about 1,400 years. How? It is a dry, almost windless climate. From the sky, these drawings are obvious and deliberate. Humans must have made them. People have photographed them from helicopters and planes. But the Native Americans who made them could not even see the finished pictures! So why—and how—did they make them?

At least 600 years ago, the beautiful city of Machu Picchu was constructed in Peru. It was built entirely of stone high in the Andes Mountains. The stones in the walls fit together so perfectly that no mortar was used. Even now, the blade of a knife cannot fit between most of these stones! These people knew that in a place that had earthquakes, mortar-free construction was sturdier than that which used mortar. But for some unknown reason, the people left. Then the city lay for years, forgotten. Its ruins were found in 1911. What happened to the people? Why did they abandon their city?

Check Your Understanding

1. The Andes Mountains
   a. have spectacular geoglyphs.
   b. have never had a city.
   c. have earthquakes.
   d. were undiscovered until 1911.

2. A **geoglyph** is a(n)
   a. earth mound in the shape of a snake, bear, or bird.
   b. ancient Native American alphabet.
   c. drawing on a cave wall.
   d. drawing on the ground.

3. Why might we never find the answers to these mysteries?
   a. There is no evidence left of Native American culture before the 1700s.
   b. Without written records, we can only guess at what happened.
   c. Today's Native Americans believe they must keep these secrets sacred.
   d. The Peruvian government will not allow anyone to study the geoglyphs or Machu Picchu.

4. People made the Nazcan Plateau lines around the year
   a. 600 CE.
   b. 800 CE.
   c. 1200 CE.
   d. 1400 CE.

/4

Warm-Up 29

Name _____

The Story of Pizza

Do you like pizza? It is one of the most popular foods in the United States. The Italians made the first pizza. In America, pizzas became popular in Chicago. In the 1890s, a man there made pizzas each day. He carried trays of pizzas on his head. He walked through Italian neighborhoods. He sold slices as he walked. His name has been lost to history.

In 1905, Gennaro Lombardi opened the first American pizzeria. Lombardi's is still selling pizzas. It is in New York City.

Somewhere in America, someone is always eating pizza. In fact, a lot of someones:

Each minute of each day, Americans eat 210,000 slices of pizza. Pepperoni is the most popular topping. The least popular is anchovies. Anchovies are tiny, salted fish. Still, enough people like it that many pizzerias offer the topping.

Pizza is popular around the world. But the toppings are not the same. The most popular toppings in Japan are eel and squid! Hawaiian pizza topped with ham and pineapple is the most popular kind in Australia. What are their other popular toppings? Bacon and egg. The Brazilians created dessert pizza. They use bananas, chocolate, and pineapple as toppings.

Check Your Understanding

1. The favorite pizza toppings in Australia are
   a. sausage and pepperoni.
   b. eel and squid.
   c. bacon and egg.
   d. pineapple and ham.

2. Anchovies are a type of
   a. fish.
   b. eel.
   c. squid.
   d. dessert.

3. In the United States, it would be odd to ask for which pizza topping?
   a. pineapple
   b. eel
   c. pepperoni
   d. ham

4. Which statement is false?
   a. Gennaro Lombardi is no longer alive.
   b. Someone in Italy created the first pizza.
   c. The first U.S. pizzeria opened in the city where pizzas first became popular.
   d. Someone in Brazil created the first dessert pizza.

/4

Warm-Up
30

Name _____

The Indy 500

Did you know that the Indianapolis Speedway is the biggest sports facility ever? On the day of the Indy 500 race, a person sits in each of its 257,000 seats. With the infield seating, a total of 400,000 people can watch. During the race, the stadium holds as many people as one of America's 100 largest cities. It is the world's biggest single-day sports event.

If you've never been there, it's hard to picture how big the Speedway is. It is huge. Yankee Stadium, the Rose Bowl, the Kentucky Derby track, Wimbledon's tennis courts, the Roman Coliseum, and Vatican City could all fit inside at once! The Speedway has a 2.5-mile oval track. It is made for cars to go fast. That is

because the Indy cars go about 185 miles per hour. The cars move so fast that their tires reach the same temperature as boiling water! That is why the drivers make so many pit stops. A pit crew changes all of a car's tires within seconds.

The first Indy 500 was held in 1911. Drivers went around the track 200 times. They went 500 miles. To save fuel, the race was not held during World Wars I and II. In 1977, Janet Guthrie was the first female driver. In 2009, a woman came in third place. That is the best finish ever for a female.

Check Your Understanding

1. The first Indianapolis 500 race was held about
    a. 25 years ago.   c. 75 years ago.
    b. 50 years ago.   d. 100 years ago.

2. There were a number of years when the Indy 500 was not held. Why?
    a. to help the environment   c. to save money
    b. to save gas   d. because people threatened to blow up the Speedway

3. What causes the tires to reach such high temperatures?
    a. a very hot and sunny day   c. very fast driving speeds
    b. the material that the track is built from   d. all car tires get that hot

4. In addition to changing tires during a race, a pit crew
    a. waxes the car.   c. repaints the car.
    b. washes the car.   d. refuels the car.

/4

Fascinating People

Name _____

Dr. Antonia Novello, Former Surgeon General

In 1990, the U.S. Surgeon General was Dr. Antonia Novello. She was the first woman to hold this job. She was the first Latina, too. The Surgeon General is the nation's main doctor. She does research. She tells the public what she finds. Novello taught about the dangers of smoking and drinking alcohol. She told the companies that make beer, wine, and cigarettes to stop trying to get teens to buy their products. She taught people how to keep from getting AIDS, too.

Novello was born in Puerto Rico. She earned a medical degree there in 1970. As a child, she always wanted to become a doctor. But she didn't know that she would one day be the most important doctor in the United States.

While growing up, Novello had a health problem. Yet, she did not get the operations she needed until she was in medical school. Even so, her grades never fell. She always did her best.

Novello was surprised when she was asked to be Surgeon General. She wasn't looking for a job. President George H. W. Bush asked her himself. She agreed. She left the job when a new president took over. She kept working to improve health care for children.

Check Your Understanding

1. Where was Dr. Novello born and raised?
   a. in South America
   b. in the United States
   c. in Puerto Rico
   d. in the Bahamas

2. How did Dr. Novello become interested in being a doctor?
   a. She wanted to be the U.S. Surgeon General.
   b. It was a childhood dream of hers.
   c. Her mother told her that she should become a doctor.
   d. President George H.W. Bush suggested it to her.

3. During medical school, Dr. Novello
   a. had operations, yet kept her grades high.
   b. was asked to be the U.S. Surgeon General.
   c. had to stop classes due to her illness.
   d. learned to speak Spanish.

4. Which statement is false?
   a. Dr. Novello was fired from her position as U.S. Surgeon General.
   b. Dr. Novello became a doctor in 1970.
   c. Dr. Novello stopped being the U.S. Surgeon General when President Bush left office.
   d. Dr. Novello was especially concerned about stopping AIDS.

/4

Warm-Up 2

Dr. Elizabeth Blackwell, First U.S. Female Doctor

Name _____

Elizabeth Blackwell moved to New York City when she was 11 years old. It was 1832. People were dying. They had cholera. Elizabeth wished she could help them get better.

When Elizabeth grew up, she nursed a friend back to health. Her friend told her to become a doctor. At that time, few women went to college. None had ever earned a medical degree. Elizabeth decided she would be the first.

She studied the same books that the medical students did. She paid doctors to teach her. Yet, when she was ready for medical school, no college would let her in. She had to plead for years to get Geneva Medical College to let her try.

Then the teachers and students were mean to her. To please her teachers, Elizabeth had to work much harder than the male students. Even so, she earned high grades.

In 1849, Elizabeth was the first woman in the United States to be a doctor. But then no one would hire her. No one would rent her office space! She didn't give up. Instead, she started the Women's Medical College. In this way, she helped other women to become doctors. In 1857, she opened a hospital. It was for poor women and children. Few of the patients could pay her. Still, Elizabeth was happy. She was helping the sick.

Check Your Understanding

1. Where did Elizabeth go to medical school?
   a. Geneva Medical College
   b. Women's Medical College
   c. Hobart and William Smith College
   d. The article does not say.

2. What did Elizabeth do in 1832?
   a. moved to New York City
   b. earned a doctor's degree
   c. opened her own hospital
   d. entered college

3. You can tell that Elizabeth was most interested in giving medical care to
   a. rich people.
   b. poor women and children.
   c. men.
   d. soldiers.

4. Which event occurred last in Elizabeth's life?
   a. She started a college.
   b. She earned a medical degree.
   c. She pleaded with Geneva Medical College.
   d. She started a hospital.

/4

Name _____

3 Sojourner Truth, Civil Rights Leader

Sojourner Truth was born a slave. Her name was Isabella. She was sold away from her parents when she was nine years old; and when she was 13, a man named John Dumont bought her. Three years later, he made her get married. He wanted her to have babies so that they would be his slaves. Isabella had five children. In 1862, her master said he would free her, but he did not stick to his word. Isabella went to Isaac Van Wagener's home. When her master came, Van Wagener paid $20 for her. Then, he set her free.

She went to see her children. Then, Dumont sold her son Peter out of state. This was against the law. Isabella took Dumont to court. The judge ruled that

Peter be brought back. He was given to Isabella. This was the first time an African American woman won a case against a white man.

Isabella had a dream in 1843. In it, she said that God told her to tell others what it was like to be a slave. She changed her name to Sojourner Truth. Then, she spoke to large crowds in many places, stressing equal rights for all.

In 1865, Sojourner got on a streetcar in the nation's capital. The streetcar conductor hit her because she would not get off! Streetcars were just for white riders. Sojourner got the streetcar company to give everyone the right to ride.

Check Your Understanding

1. What was Sojourner's name at birth?
   a. Sojourner
   b. Isabella
   c. Peter
   d. Truth

2. How many times was Sojourner sold?
   a. never
   b. once
   c. twice
   d. three times

3. What was Sojourner the first African American woman to do?
   a. be freed from slavery
   b. ride a streetcar
   c. win a court case against a white man
   d. have babies that would belong to her master

4. Why did Sojourner address large crowds?
   a. She wanted to get her son back.
   b. She believed that it was what God wanted her to do.
   c. She wanted to ride streetcars in peace.
   d. She hoped to make the price of slaves less affordable.

/4

Warm-Up
4

The Angel of Marye's Heights

Name _____

Richard Rowland Kirkland was born in South Carolina in 1843. When he was 17 years old, the southern states withdrew from the Union. They said they were a separate nation called the Confederate States of America. The Union went to war with the Confederacy. This began the U.S. Civil War.

Richard joined the Confederate army. In December 1862, he fought at the Battle of Fredericksburg. In a place called Marye's Heights, thousands of Union troops ran uphill against enemy fire. Richard and his army shot at them from behind a stone wall. The Union soldiers didn't stand a chance.

Hundreds of Union men lay wounded. They screamed for help. This went on all night. No one dared to help them. No one wanted to be shot. In the morning, Richard could stand no more. He was afraid. Still, he climbed over the wall. He brought water and blankets to the injured and dying. It did not matter that they were on opposite sides in the war. He could not bear for them to suffer.

Both the Yankees and his own army cheered for Richard. They were proud of his kind actions. Less than a year later, Richard died in battle. He was just 20 years old. Today a statue of him stands in front of the stone wall.

Check Your Understanding

1. After December 1862, Richard was known as the
   a. "Pride of the Confederacy."
   b. "Helper of Marye's Heights."
   c. "Winner of the Battle of Fredericksburg."
   d. "Angel of Marye's Heights."

2. Why were there so many wounded Union soldiers after the battle?
   a. The Union troops were in the open, and the Confederates were behind a stone wall.
   b. The Union troops were new soldiers who hadn't been trained how to fight.
   c. The Union troops had no weapons.
   d. The Union troops had gotten separated from their leaders.

3. You can tell that Yankees were people
   a. whose job was to take care of the wounded after a battle.
   b. who were neutral and didn't take sides in the war.
   c. fighting for the Confederacy.
   d. fighting for the Union.

4. The Richard Rowland Kirkland statue is in front of the stone wall because he
   a. brought about an end to the Civil War there.
   b. took action that made the Confederates win the battle there.
   c. showed mercy to enemy soldiers there.
   d. died taking care of wounded men there.

/4

Warm-Up

5

Barbara Jordan, Former U.S. Congresswoman

Name _____

Barbara Jordan was born in 1936. She grew up poor. She worked hard. She earned a law degree. In 1966, she became the first African American woman to go to the Texas Senate. She did well there.

In 1972, Jordan was one of the first African American women sent to the House of Representatives. She became an important voice for poor people. She made sure that everyone had a chance to vote. She voted for a law to **benefit** hurt workers. She helped to pass laws to give kids free school lunches. Jordan was well liked. In a poll, people chose her as the woman they most wanted as president. But it was not to be. She got a serious illness in 1973. It is called multiple sclerosis. It makes a person get more and more weak.

Jordan was a great speaker. She was the first African American woman to give the keynote address at a Democratic National Convention. It was in 1976. Historians say her speech was one of the best of the 20th century. She was a keynote speaker at the 1992 Democratic National Convention, too. Most of her speeches appear in *Barbara Jordan: Speaking the Truth with Eloquent Thunder*.

Jordan was given the U.S. Medal of Freedom. That is the highest honor the U.S. government can grant a citizen. She died in 1996.

Check Your Understanding

1. Jordan was the first African American woman ever to
   a. be elected to the U.S. Senate.
   b. join the U.S. House of Representatives.
   c. be the U.S. president.
   d. give the keynote speech at the Democratic National Convention.

2. Why was Jordan probably such a good voice for the poor?
   a. They marched around her house with signs.
   b. They had given money to her campaign.
   c. She had once been poor and understood their needs.
   d. She had multiple sclerosis.

3. What is another word for **benefit**?
   a. hire   c. charge
   b. help   d. medicate

4. While Jordan was in the House of Representatives, she was a member of
   a. Congress.   c. the military.
   b. the president's cabinet.   d. the Texas Senate.

/4

Warm-Up
6

Name _____

Garrett Morgan, Inventor

Garrett Morgan was born in 1877 to a former slave. When he reached 14, he needed to help support his family. So he left school to work as a handyman. Although he only finished sixth grade, Morgan was very smart. He invented two important things still used today.

In 1914, Morgan made the first gas mask. He called it a safety hood. It let a person breathe clean air even in the midst of deadly fumes. He showed it to several companies. But no one believed it would really work. Then in 1916, there was an explosion in a tunnel 282 feet underground. Smoke, dust, and natural gas fumes filled the tunnel. Several firefighters who tried to get to the trapped men were killed. No one could safely go into the tunnel to help them escape.

Morgan heard about the accident. He rushed to the scene. He and his brother Frank put on gas masks. They went down into the tunnel. Together, they saved 32 workers' lives. After that, orders poured in for gas masks. Over time, gas masks became standard equipment for soldiers, firefighters, and police officers.

One day, Morgan saw a bad crash at a city **intersection**. It really upset him. He wanted to keep other people from crashing. But how? There just weren't enough police to direct traffic at every busy intersection. Morgan thought and thought. Then he designed the first traffic light in 1923. Morgan's light only had a red and a green light. But his basic design still directs our traffic.

Check Your Understanding

1. Garrett Morgan invented
   a. traffic lights.
   b. shovels.
   c. intersections.
   d. mining tunnels.

2. When did Garrett Morgan's fortune change for the better?
   a. after he saw a bad car crash
   b. once he became a handyman
   c. as soon as he invented the safety hood
   d. after he helped to save 32 trapped men

3. At an **intersection**,
   a. two countries share a border.
   b. there is a traffic circle.
   c. two or more roads meet.
   d. people disagree on which way to turn.

4. How did Garrett Morgan's safety hood help people?
   a. It kept them free from burns.
   b. It kept them from breathing dangerous fumes.
   c. It gave them fresh oxygen from a tank.
   d. It prevented car crashes.

/4

Warm-Up 7

Name _____

Mary McLeod Bethune, Educator

Mary McLeod Bethune was born in 1875. She was the fifteenth of 17 children. Her parents were freed slaves. They had a tiny cabin in South Carolina. Mary wanted to learn. But no school would take her. When she was 11, a school opened five miles away. She walked there and back each day. She taught what she learned to her siblings.

When she grew up, she wanted to help others. So she opened an African American girls' school in 1904. It was in Daytona Beach, Florida. Soon it merged with a boys' college to become Bethune-Cookman University. In 1923, Mary became the college president. She served in that role for 20 years.

Back then, there were no female college presidents. But Mary didn't let that stop her.

Mary wanted to prove that black students could do just as well as white students. She was close friends with First Lady Eleanor Roosevelt. This helped to make her college well known. Mary opened it to tourists. She made people proud of what her students had achieved.

Mary had the amazing ability to turn hatred into friendship. When a white man threatened to shoot one of her students, Mary spoke to him with kindness. He gave money to her school. When blacks were kept off the beach, Mary bought a stretch of beach and opened it to everyone.

Check Your Understanding

1. Mary was born in
   a. South Carolina.
   b. North Carolina.
   c. Florida.
   d. Washington, D.C.

2. Which event occurred third?
   a. Mary taught her siblings what she learned in school.
   b. Bethune-Cookman University formed.
   c. Mary was a college president.
   d. Mary opened an African American girls' school.

3. How did being friends with the First Lady help Mary's school?
   a. The First Lady made Congress give money to the school.
   b. The First Lady didn't want anyone to know about the school.
   c. The First Lady told many others about the school.
   d. The First Lady told the president that she liked the school.

4. How did Mary handle prejudice toward her students?
   a. She took the people who were acting prejudiced to court.
   b. She made the people who were acting prejudiced work at her school.
   c. She bought a beach and gave it to the people who were acting prejudiced.
   d. She was so kind to the people who were acting prejudiced that she won them over.

/4

Warm-Up 8

Name _____

Will Cross, Adventurer

Most of what you eat is carbohydrates. Your body breaks them down into sugar. The sugar is used for energy. But people with diabetes cannot do this. Their bodies do not change sugar into energy. Without treatment, diabetes can lead to blindness, heart disease, and even death. Millions of people around the world have diabetes.

Fred Banting was a Canadian doctor. He found out how to make insulin. He took insulin from dogs. He made a shot. When **diabetics** took the shot, it helped their bodies to use sugar. It let them be healthier and live longer. In 1923, Fred won the Nobel Prize in medicine. He saved millions of lives. And he made new things possible for people with diabetes.

Will Cross is an American mountain climber. He has had diabetes since he was a child. He decided that he would not let it hold him back. He has shown that anything is possible. He manages his condition in tough situations. When he climbs mountains, he faces extreme temperatures and gets tired. Yet Will has climbed the highest peaks on each continent. He is the first person with diabetes to do this. He has hiked to both the North and South Poles and led trips to 15 unmapped mountains, too. Will tells diabetics that they can live life to the fullest. He is living proof.

Check Your Understanding

1. Your body changes carbohydrates into
   a. protein.
   b. sugar.
   c. fat.
   d. vitamins.

2. A **diabetic** is a person who
   a. climbs mountains.
   b. wins a Nobel Prize in medicine.
   c. has a disease called insulin.
   d. has a disease called diabetes.

3. Fred Banting
   a. helped many people with diabetes.
   b. climbed the highest peaks on each continent.
   c. cured diabetes.
   d. hiked to both Poles.

4. Will Cross wants to
   a. hike to both the North and South Poles.
   b. climb the highest peaks on each continent.
   c. encourage diabetics to do great things.
   d. market a new kind of insulin.

/4

Name _____

Louis Pasteur, the Milk Man

Louis Pasteur lived long ago, but the things he did help keep you healthy today. He was not a medical doctor. Yet he found new ways to help keep people from getting ill. Pasteur studied germs and figured out that germs could live almost anywhere. He thought that these germs caused sickness.

Pasteur proved that sicknesses happen when germs get inside a body and multiply. He also found that if a few weak germs were put into an animal, the animal's body would develop its own defense against the germ.

In 1881, he began work on a **vaccine** to stop rabies. Four years later, a rabid dog bit a boy. The parents begged Pasteur to save their son. Pasteur did not want to use his shot on a person. He did not know what would happen, but he was sure that the boy was going to die without it. The shot was his only chance. So Pasteur gave him the shot. The little boy lived!

Pasteur found a way to keep milk free of germs, too. He learned that germs could not stand heat. When he heated milk to 140°F, then quickly cooled it and sealed it in clean jars, the germs died. His method is called *pasteurization*. Milk has been pasteurized ever since.

Check Your Understanding

1. What is another word for vaccine?
   a. vitamin
   b. pill
   c. prescription
   d. shot

2. How does a vaccine work?
   a. It kills germs as they enter the body.
   b. It doesn't let germs get into the body.
   c. It helps the body make a defense against germs.
   d. It makes the body produce more red blood cells.

3. What happened last?
   a. A rabid dog bit a boy.
   b. Pasteur gave a boy a vaccine.
   c. Pasteur developed a rabies shot.
   d. The parents begged Pasteur to help.

4. Why does a pasteurized liquid need to be sealed in a clean jar?
   a. to be sure that no germs are already in the jar or can get into the jar
   b. to be sure that the germs cannot get the air they need to breathe
   c. to keep the liquid the right temperature
   d. to make the liquid taste better

/4

Warm-Up
10

Name _____

The First Woman in Space

The first female astronaut blasted off on June 16, 1963. Her title was *cosmonaut*. (That's what the Soviet space program calls its astronauts). Her name was Valentina Tereshkova.

When she was just two years old, Valentina's father died. He was killed in World War II. This left her family very poor. At 17, she went to work in a factory to help support the family. She went to school at night, too. She joined an air sports club. She learned how to jump from planes with a parachute.

Valentina wanted to be a cosmonaut. She wrote to the space program and volunteered. What she lacked in education, she made up for in passion.

Her desire and her ability to parachute got her accepted. She was thrilled to be chosen as the first woman to go into space.

Valentina got into the *Vostok 6* capsule and went into orbit. Using a radio, she talked with another cosmonaut who was orbiting Earth in another spaceship. She did tests on herself. The Soviets wanted to know how a female body reacted to being in space. Valentina spent almost 71 hours in space. When she was four miles above Earth's surface, she ejected. She parachuted to the ground. A few years later, she left the cosmonaut corps. She went into politics.

The United States did not send a woman into space until 1983.

Check Your Understanding

1. The Soviet people who go into space are called
   a. astronauts.
   b. aeronauts.
   c. cosmonauts.
   d. tereshkovas.

2. Valentina was selected to go into space because
   a. she had a college education.
   b. she knew how to parachute.
   c. she worked in a factory.
   d. her father had been a famous cosmonaut.

3. How many years passed between the first Soviet female in space and the first American female in space?
   a. 5 years
   b. 10 years
   c. 20 years
   d. 25 years

4. To return from space, Valentina had to
   a. be a skilled pilot.
   b. do math calculations perfectly in order to know when to release the landing gear.
   c. land in the ocean and swim to shore.
   d. parachute from the spacecraft when she was a few miles above Earth.

/4

Warm-Up 11

Name _____

I. M. Pei, Architect

Ieoh Ming Pei was born in China in 1917. His parents sent him to school in America. His father wanted him to be a doctor. Instead he earned a degree in architecture from MIT (Massachusetts Institute of Technology). This meant he designed buildings. He was soon one of the best-known **architects** in the world. He is a master of modern architecture.

During college, his friends called him I. M. He has used that name ever since. He married Eileen Loo and had four children. In 1954, the whole family became U.S. citizens. One year later, he opened his own firm.

I. M. Pei made unique designs. When creating additions for existing buildings, he blended the new with the old. He designed an addition for the Louvre Art Museum in France. The Louvre was a palace built 800 years ago. At first, the French people did not like the idea of an addition. But when they saw Pei's clever design, they knew that the old building would look even better. During construction, digging uncovered some old castle walls. No one had known they were there. So, Pei changed his plans to make the walls a part of a display in the museum.

Some of Pei's other famous works include the JFK Library, Dallas City Hall, and the Bank of China Tower. In 1983, he won the highest prize in architecture.

Check Your Understanding

1. In 1955, I. M. Pei
   a. was born.
   b. won an architecture prize.
   c. became a U.S. citizen.
   d. started his own firm.

2. An **architect** is a person who
   a. wins awards.
   b. comes from China.
   c. designs structures.
   d. digs the foundation of buildings.

3. Why did Pei change his original plans for the Louvre?
   a. He wanted to please the people who were opposed to his designs.
   b. He decided to add old castle walls into the design.
   c. He needed to save money because he was going over budget.
   d. He was in a hurry to move on to his next project.

4. Which statement is false?
   a. I. M. Pei designed the Louvre.
   b. I. M. Pei received the highest prize an architect can earn.
   c. I. M. Pei designed the Bank of China Tower.
   d. I. M. Pei became a U.S. citizen when he was about 37 years old.

/4

Warm-Up

12   Delvin Miller, Harness Racing Master

Name _____

Delvin Miller was born in 1913. He lived for 83 years. He loved horses every moment of his life. While he was still a teen, he competed in harness races. This means that he drove horses in a sulky. It is a tiny cart with two bicycle wheels. He guided his standard bred horse around a track to **victory**. He won his first race at the age of 16.

Delvin helped to change horse racing. He supported the use of moving starting gates. (They are now standard.) He urged drivers to wear safety helmets in races. He built a new track. It had a man-made, rubber-like surface. It is called The Meadows.

Delvin decided to breed racehorses. In 1948, he bought Adios. He was a champion male racehorse. Many say that Adios was the greatest stud in harness racing history. He fathered eight champions and 581 other racehorses!

As a driver, Delvin won the Hambletonian trotting race in 1950. As a trainer, he won again in 1953 and 1961. It is harness racing's biggest win. But Delvin was always winning races. In fact, he won his last race just three months before he died! During his career, he drove 2,058 horses. They won more than $11 million.

Check Your Understanding

1. The Meadows is a
  a. trotting race.
  b. stable for horses.
  c. racetrack.
  d. moving starting gate.

2. An antonym for **victory** is
  a. acceptance.
  b. defeat.
  c. training.
  d. win.

3. Adios was the father of
  a. many race horses.
  b. two famous harness race drivers.
  c. Delvin Miller.
  d. the sport of harness racing.

4. Delvin Miller died in
  a. 1953.
  b. 1961.
  c. 1983.
  d. 1996.

/4

Name _____

Asa Philip Randolph, Civil Rights Leader

Asa Philip Randolph worked for more than 40 years for equal rights for African American workers. In the 1920s, men worked on trains as conductors. They formed a big black labor union. They made Asa their leader. He negotiated with the rail companies. He got $2 million worth of pay increases for the workers. He got a shorter workweek and paid overtime.

In 1940, many companies would not hire black workers. And even if a black man got a job, he could not move up to a better one. Asa knew this was wrong. He wanted things changed. He went to see President Roosevelt. He asked him to end the unfair treatment. But Roosevelt did not act. So, Asa said that he would get 100,000 people. They would march to the White House. They would protest. Then everyone would know about the problem.

In June 1941, Roosevelt signed a law. It said that a person could not be kept from a job due to race, color, faith, or national origin. The law applied just to the government and companies that made war supplies. Still, it was a step forward. The next year Asa won a major award. It came from the NAACP (National Association for the Advancement of Colored People).

Check Your Understanding

1. When President Roosevelt signed the bill in 1941, he
 a. ended all discrimination against African Americans.
 b. made job discrimination illegal in the United States.
 c. made job discrimination illegal in the government.
 d. made sure African Americans would get better educations.

2. The word **negotiated** means
 a. bargained.   c. argued.
 b. threatened.   d. reorganized.

3. Why did the NAACP give Asa its highest award?
 a. He organized a march on Washington, D.C.
 b. He led the biggest black labor union.
 c. He was the vice president of America's largest labor union.
 d. He helped to bring about a law that helped African American workers.

4. Why did Randolph want African Americans to march in Washington, D.C.?
 a. He wanted to cause trouble for the unions.
 b. He wanted the nation to know that African Americans faced discrimination.
 c. He hoped that the march would bring him a lot of fame and money.
 d. He wanted African Americans to spend time with each other in the capital.

/4

Warm-Up

14   Jason McElwain, Basketball Star

Name _____

Jason McElwain is better known as J-Mac. He has a disability called *autism*. It can make learning difficult. It makes it hard for him to understand social clues, too. For example, he may not understand when someone is happy or sad or be able to react in an appropriate way.

J-Mac went to Greece Athena High School in Rochester, New York. He loved basketball. Jim Johnson, his basketball coach, made J-Mac manager of the team. Everyone thought he was too short to play. However, he played during the last game of his senior year in high school. And no one who was there will ever forget what happened.

On February 15, 2006, J-Mac's school was playing another school for a division title. Greece had a big lead. So Johnson sent J-Mac in to play the final four minutes. J-Mac threw two shots and missed. But then, he made six 3-point shots and one 2-point shot. The final buzzer rang. J-Mac had scored 20 points in less than four minutes! The crowd stormed the basketball court. Everyone was cheering. J-Mac's teammates carried him off the court on their shoulders.

J-Mac's amazing feat made national news. He won an ESPY Award for the Best Moment in Sports in 2006. He had shown that a disability doesn't have to hold one back from doing amazing things.

Check Your Understanding

1. J-Mac's autism caused him to
   a. be unable to speak.
   b. struggle to understand social situations.
   c. be unable to play sports.
   d. become a movie star.

2. Which event happened third?
   a. J-Mac made seven shots.
   b. J-Mac missed two shots.
   c. J-Mac became team manager.
   d. J-Mac won a famous award.

3. Everyone was surprised by what J-Mac did because
   a. he couldn't see the basketball hoop for which he was aiming.
   b. it's amazing for anyone to make that many baskets so fast.
   c. they didn't know he knew how to play basketball.
   d. the other team just stood there and let him make a lot of points.

4. It is clear that J-Mac had
   a. never played basketball before.
   b. not watched televised basketball games.
   c. been the school's most valuable player the entire season.
   d. been practicing basketball in his spare time.

/4

Warm-Up
15 Loreta Velasquez, Civil War Soldier

Name _____

Loreta Velasquez was born in New Orleans. She was the daughter of a Spanish diplomat. When she was 14, she married an army officer. William joined the Confederate troops during the Civil War. Loreta wanted to join him in battle. He said no. So Loreta **recruited** 236 men. She sent them to fight beside her spouse.

Loreta's husband died in a training accident. She decided to fight in the war. She put on a fake beard and mustache. She was thin, so she made a padded jacket. Wearing it made her look like she had muscles. She enlisted to fight in the Confederate Army. The year was 1860. She was a member of troops from Arkansas. She used the name Harry T. Buford.

"Harry" fought in three big battles. Then, in 1862, she was shot. Her secret was revealed. The Confederate Army sent her home. However, Loreta re-enlisted. This time she joined the 21st Louisiana Infantry. She fought in another big battle. This time she fought with the men she had helped to recruit. Someone told an officer that she was a woman. Her secret was out again! So, Loreta became a spy for the South.

Loreta wrote a book in 1876. Its title is *The Woman in Battle*. In it, she tells about her life and the battles in which she fought.

Check Your Understanding

1. Loreta got married when she was just
   a. 13 years old.
   b. 14 years old.
   c. 15 years old.
   d. 17 years old.

2. The word **recruited** means _____ to serve in the armed forces.
   a. hired
   b. begged
   c. signed up
   d. trained

3. Loreta's husband's first name was
   a. William.
   b. Harry.
   c. Louis.
   d. Buford.

4. What did Loreta do during the Civil War?
   a. She was a Union soldier and spy.
   b. She was a Confederate soldier and spy.
   c. She was a nurse for the Union troops.
   d. She was a nurse for the Confederate troops.

/4

16   Clara Hale's House

Name _____

Clara Hale was an African American. In 1932, her husband died. She needed to take care of her three children and earn a living. So Clara opened a home day care center. She took in foster children, too. People soon saw that Clara had a special quality. She loved all children.

Clara retired in 1968. But she didn't get to relax long. Her daughter gave her a new mission. Beginning in 1969, Clara started Hale House. It is a home for children whose mothers use drugs. It is for babies born addicted to drugs, too.

Lorraine Hale was Clara's daughter. She saw an addict sleeping in a park. She had a baby. Lorraine told the woman to go to Clara for help. The young woman did so.

She told other drug-addicted women that Clara would care for their kids while they got treatment. Soon Clara had 22 children in her care. At first, her grown children worked overtime to pay for the kids' expenses.

Then, Clara received some money from the city of New York. She bought a big home in 1975. It quickly filled with children. In 1985, Hale House got national attention and more money. Clara lived to be 87. She worked until she died in 1992. Hale House had already helped more than 1,000 children.

Check Your Understanding

1. In what year did Hale House get national recognition?
     a. 1969   c. 1985
     b. 1975   d. 1992

2. Which event occurred second in Clara's life?
     a. Clara ran a home day care.
     b. Clara retired.
     c. Clara took care of children whose mothers were addicted to drugs.
     d. Clara bought a large home and called it Hale House.

3. How did Clara help drug-addicted women?
     a. She took care of their children while they got help for their problems.
     b. She took their children away and gave them to new families.
     c. She left the children in their mothers' care and counseled the women.
     d. She adopted their babies herself.

4. In what year was Clara Hale born?
     a. 1900   c. 1905
     b. 1903   d. 1932

/4

Warm-Up
17

Name _____

Wilma Mankiller, Former Cherokee Chief

Wilma Mankiller was a Cherokee Native American. Her tribe is the largest in the United States. She was born in 1945. Her family was poor. They had 11 children. When she grew up, she went to college. Wilma knew that she wanted to serve her tribe.

A tribe's leader is called the chief. In 1983, Ross Swimmer ran for chief. Wilma ran as his deputy chief. (That means she would be second in command.) During the race, she got angry letters and phone calls. Someone cut her car tires. Many men did not want her as deputy chief. Even so, Ross was elected. Wilma stood at his side. Two years later, Ross left his post. Wilma took over. She was the first woman to be the chief of the Cherokee Nation.

As chief, Wilma built health clinics. She improved the justice system. She helped tribe members to get indoor plumbing. She worked to save the history and customs of the Cherokee. She was the chief until 1995. She stayed at her post through two life-threatening illnesses and a kidney transplant.

Wilma was added into the National Women's Hall of Fame in 1993. She received the Presidential Medal of Freedom in 1998. It is the highest award the U.S. government can give to a citizen. She died in 2010.

Check Your Understanding

1. In the United States, the Cherokee Nation is the
  a. smallest tribe.
  b. second biggest tribe.
  c. third biggest tribe.
  d. biggest tribe.

2. Which event occurred third?
  a. Wilma was added to the National Women's Hall of Fame.
  b. Wilma was elected as Cherokee Nation Chief.
  c. Wilma received the Presidential Medal of Freedom.
  d. Wilma went to college.

3. Complete this analogy: *president* is to *vice president* as *chief* is to
  a. *vice chief.*
  b. *Wilma Mankiller.*
  c. *deputy chief.*
  d. *Cherokee.*

4. How did the Cherokee tribe benefit by having Wilma Mankiller as its chief?
  a. She got federal aid for the Cherokee nation.
  b. She made Cherokee tribe members into U.S. citizens.
  c. She got national recognition for Cherokee problems.
  d. She made improvements in the lives of the citizens.

/4

Name _____

18   Dr. Susan La Flesche Picotte

Susan La Flesche Picotte was born in 1865. Her father, Iron Eye, was the last Omaha chief in Nebraska. He wanted her to fit into white society. So, he gave her a white name. She grew up on a reservation. As a child, she saw a sick Native American woman die. The local white doctor would not treat her! Susan was horrified. She decided that she would be a doctor. She would take care of her people.

When Susan grew up, she went to a college for non-whites. It was in Pennsylvania. There, she told a woman doctor about her goal. Dr. Martha Waldron helped Susan to apply for a scholarship. If she won, the money would pay for her education. Susan did win.

And she was smart. She finished the three-year course in just two years. Susan became the first Native American woman to earn a medical degree in the United States.

She married her husband, Henry Picotte, and the pair moved back to Nebraska. First, she spent time traveling the Omaha Reservation. She made house calls for the sick. They had no way to come to her. Then, she worked as the doctor for 1,200 children. They lived at a boarding school. In 1913, she saw a lifelong dream fulfilled. She opened a hospital on a reservation in Walthill, Nebraska. She died two years later.

Check Your Understanding

1. Susan La Flesche Picotte was the first Native American woman to
   a. be the chief of the Omaha tribe.
   b. win a scholarship to medical school.
   c. work in a hospital in Nebraska.
   d. become a doctor in the United States.

2. Susan decided what she wanted to do after she
   a. saw a woman die from lack of medical care.
   b. won a scholarship to medical school.
   c. married Henry Picotte.
   d. met Dr. Martha Waldron.

3. Susan attended college
   a. on the reservation.
   b. in Pennsylvania.
   c. in Nebraska.
   d. in Omaha.

4. About how old was Susan when she died?
   a. 46
   b. 48
   c. 50
   d. 52

/4

Warm-Up

19   William Wilberforce, British Abolitionist

In the 1700s, Great Britain had a large empire. It owned colonies all over the world. The British colonies had slaves. British ships carried slaves kidnapped in Africa to these colonies.

William Wilberforce was a young British politician in the House of Commons. One day, William had a religious **conversion**. This means that his faith changed. After that, he looked at things differently. He wanted to change laws to help the poor.

Some of William's friends knew that the slave trade was wrong. One of them was Thomas Clarkson. He urged William to end slavery. So, William worked to make the slave trade illegal. He tried to get other politicians to agree with him. He wrote

books. It took him 21 years to make a difference. In 1807, the British Parliament made buying and selling slaves against the law.

That was a big triumph. Yet it was still legal to own slaves. William's work was not done. He worked to make all slavery illegal. He kept working for another 21 years. Then he retired from politics. Slavery was still legal. William did not give up. He kept speaking and writing against slavery. At last, in 1833, when William was 74 years old, Parliament passed a new law. It made slavery illegal in Britain and all its colonies. William's life work was done. Three days later, he died at peace.

Check Your Understanding

1. William Wilberforce worked for most of his life to get
   a. better health care for slaves.
   b. slavery outlawed.
   c. slaves to change their faith.
   d. British colonies the ability to own slaves.

2. A **conversion** is a(n)
   a. end to the slave trade.
   b. voting practice in the British House of Commons.
   c. place where slaves are sold.
   d. change in one's point of view.

3. William died when he was
   a. 47 years old.
   b. 59 years old.
   c. 74 years old.
   d. 75 years old.

4. Why wasn't the 1807 law enough to please William?
   a. It did not stop slave owners from breaking up families by selling members.
   b. It did not pay slave owners money for their freed slaves.
   c. It did not free people who were already slaves.
   d. It did not offer slaves enough pay for their labor.

/4

Name _____

Bethany Hamilton, Fearless Surfer

Bethany Hamilton was born in 1990. Her parents and brothers were surfers. They all rode the waves in Hawaii. As a child, Bethany showed a lot of promise. She competed in the National Scholastic Surfing Association (NSSA). She did well. Rip Curl is a surfboard company. It chose to sponsor her. She was on her way to being a professional surfer. That was her dream.

Then, in 2003, tragedy struck. Bethany was lying on her surfboard. Her left arm hung down in the water. A tiger shark grabbed her. It bit off her arm just below the shoulder. If the shark had bitten two inches higher, it would have opened a major artery. There is no way she could have survived. As it was, Bethany lost about 60 percent of the blood in her body. Friends pulled her ashore. They rushed her to the hospital.

From the moment she woke up in the hospital, Bethany wanted to keep surfing. Just one month later, she was back on her board! She taught herself to surf with one arm. Then, she began competing again. In 2005, Bethany won first place in the NSSA National Championships. In 2008, she started competing full time. She took third place in her first competition against the world's best women surfers!

Check Your Understanding

1. Most likely, why did the tiger shark attack Bethany?
   a. It wanted to ruin her chances as a surfer.
   b. Another surfer who was jealous of Bethany's skill sent the shark after her.
   c. It wanted a meal.
   d. It hated humans.

2. NSSA is an acronym for
   a. National Scholastic Surfing Association.
   b. Rip Curl's highest award.
   c. National Shore Surfers Association.
   d. National Southern Surfers Association.

3. About how many years after the attack did Bethany start to compete in surfing full time?
   a. 3
   b. 5
   c. 8
   d. 10

4. Why does the passage title call Bethany fearless?
   a. She kept surfing after losing her arm in a terrifying attack.
   b. She lost 60 percent of the blood in her body but still survived.
   c. She is not afraid to surf even though she's taken some bad falls.
   d. She punched a tiger shark that tried to attack her.

/4

Warm-Up

21

Name _____

Mother Jones, Labor Activitist

In 1903, a group of textile (cloth) workers and children marched in protest to the home of President Theodore Roosevelt. Many in the group had missing fingers and mangled hands from accidents with the machines in the textile mills where they worked 60 hours each week. The leader of the group was a short woman. She had gray hair and a black bonnet. Her name was Mother Jones.

Mother Jones was born Mary Harris in Ireland in 1837. Her father moved to America. When she grew up, she married George Jones. But yellow fever struck her family. Her husband and all four of her kids died in the **epidemic**.

Mother Jones moved to Chicago. She opened a shop and made dresses. A fire swept through the city. Mother Jones lost all she owned. She started to go to the Knights of Labor meetings. This was a group of working people. They did dangerous jobs for low pay. Mother Jones started to speak out against unsafe working conditions and she wanted fair wages.

Mother Jones spent 59 years helping child workers, miners, garment workers, and trash workers. Because she would not give up, the press called her the most dangerous woman in America. When she died at the age of 93, she was planning a coal mine strike.

Check Your Understanding

1. For 59 years, Mother Jones fought to get workers
   a. jobs.
   b. freedom from epidemics.
   c. retirement plans.
   d. fair wages and safe working conditions.

2. An **epidemic** is
   a. the rapid spread of disease.
   b. a textile mill.
   c. a massive fire that spreads quickly.
   d. a deadly accident.

3. You can tell that in 1903
   a. there was a cure for yellow fever.
   b. it was dangerous to work in a textile mill.
   c. textile mill employees worked 40 hours a week.
   d. President Roosevelt was on Mother Jones' side.

4. Mother Jones died in
   a. 1903.
   b. 1920.
   c. 1930.
   d. 1962.

/4

Warm-Up 22

The Wizard of Menlo Park

Name _____

Thomas Edison was born in 1847. He grew up to be one of the greatest inventors to ever live. When he was 16, he did experiments on telegraph equipment. People sent telegrams using a telegraph. (A telegram was the ancestor of an e-mail.) Edison found a way to send four messages at once. Soon, Alexander Graham Bell made a crude telephone. Within a year, Edison had improved it. Edison used the money he made from his inventions to pay for the creation of more inventions. By the age of 45, he was a millionaire.

In 1876, Edison set up the world's first industrial research lab. It was at Menlo Park in New Jersey. This led to the phonograph. (It was an ancestor of a CD player.) He was the first person to record and store sounds. People called him the Wizard of Menlo Park.

Next, Edison made an electric light bulb. Then, in 1882, he opened the world's first electric power plant. It was the Pearl Street Station in New York City. It used steam to make electric power. Wires carried the power from the plant to businesses and homes. Within ten years, many places had built power plants based on his design.

In all, Edison patented 1,093 inventions. That's the most the U.S. Patent Office has ever issued to one person.

Check Your Understanding

1. What statement is true about Thomas Edison?
   a. He was the first U.S. telegraph operator.
   b. He invented nuclear power plants.
   c. He is the holder of the most U.S. patents.
   d. He was the first deaf person to create a video recording.

2. Edison's nickname stems from
   a. the name of his electric power plant.
   b. the location of his research lab.
   c. his childhood nickname.
   d. his most famous invention.

3. Which of the following items did Thomas Edison *not* invent?
   a. electric light bulbs   c. electric power plant
   b. phonographs   d. television

4. Complete this analogy: *telegram* is to *e-mail* as *phonograph* is to
   a. *CD player.*   c. *electric power plant.*
   b. *electric light bulb.*   d. *industrial research lab.*

/4

Name _____

Margaret Bourke-White, Photographer

Margaret Bourke-White was born in 1904. Her dad liked to take photos. As a child, she shared his hobby. She liked snakes, too. She went to college to learn about them. But her love of taking pictures won out. She earned a degree in 1927. Her first job was taking photos in steel mills. A magazine publisher saw her pictures. He asked her to work for him.

Margaret never let anything get in the way of a great shot. She was fearless. She hung out of helicopters. She snowshoed to logging camps. She crept through jungles. She crawled out on a windowsill of the Chrysler Building. She took photos of the street 800 feet below!

In the 1930s, Margaret worked for *Fortune* and *Life* magazines. She went to North Africa in World War II. She was the first female to photograph battles. She recorded the bombing of Russia. She photographed the Allied invasion of Italy. She was with the U.S. troops when they freed the Nazi death camps victims. The *Life* staff called her "Maggie the Indestructible."

Margaret traveled to many nations. She was the first foreign photographer to take motion pictures inside the Soviet Union. She took her favorite picture during the Korean War. It was of a returning soldier greeting his mother. The mother had been told he was dead.

Margaret died in 1971. Her photos are on display in major art museums.

Check Your Understanding

1. When did Margaret earn her college degree?
   a. 1904
   b. 1927
   c. 1930
   d. 1942

2. Which war did Margaret photograph?
   a. Civil War
   b. World War I
   c. World War II
   d. Persian Gulf War

3. For which magazine did Margaret work?
   a. *Time*
   b. *Reader's Digest*
   c. *People*
   d. *Life*

4. Why did her coworkers called her "Maggie the Indestructible"?
   a. She handled dangerous snakes.
   b. She fell from a dangerous height without breaking any bones.
   c. She went on assignment to many dangerous places.
   d. She survived three car accidents.

/4

Warm-Up 24

Terry Fox's Marathon of Hope

Name _____

Cancer is a disease. It causes tumors. It can kill. Terry Fox, a young Canadian, had cancer. He did something amazing to raise money for cancer research. In 1977, Terry was a teenager. He was told that he had bone cancer in his right leg. The doctors removed his leg above the knee. Terry had to learn to walk with an **artificial** leg. Over time, he even learned to run with it.

In April 1980, Terry began the Marathon of Hope. He started running in St. John's, Newfoundland. It is on the East Coast. He planned to run a marathon length every day all the way across Canada. That's 26 miles a day! People donated money to him, and he gave it to cancer research.

In all, Terry ran for 143 days. He ran through all sorts of weather. He ran in hail, snow, and high heat. He ran 3,280 miles. On September 1, he had to stop near Thunder Bay, Ontario. He went to the hospital. He never returned to his marathon. He died 10 months later. However, his run had raised $25 million for cancer research. Now the Marathon of Hope is run each year in his memory.

In 1985, another cancer amputee ran the whole way across Canada. Steve Fonyo was 19. He ran 4,924 miles. It took him 14 months.

Check Your Understanding

1. How many total miles did Terry run?
   a. 1, 977
   b. 3,280
   c. 4,924
   d. 5,280

2. The word **artificial** means
   a. transplanted.
   b. painted.
   c. natural.
   d. human-made.

3. Where did Terry start his run?
   a. St. John's
   b. Thunder Bay
   c. Ontario
   d. Montreal

4. Why did Terry name his run Marathon of Hope?
   a. He hoped to be the fastest marathon runner.
   b. He hoped to live in a town named Marathon in Greece.
   c. He hoped to raise money for cancer research.
   d. He hoped to honor his sister Mara.

/4

Warm-Up
25

Name _____

Nelson Mandela, South African Leader

Nelson Mandela spent over 27 years in jail. He worked on a labor crew. He could not get mail. Since the prison was more than 900 miles away from his home, he rarely saw his family.

What was this man's crime? Nelson was a black South African. He had spoken out against apartheid. Apartheid was the forced separation of whites and blacks. A white minority government ruled South Africa. Millions of black Africans could not vote. They could not go to the same schools as whites. They could not live in the same places. They could only sit in certain seats on buses or trains. Nelson said that all people were equal. They should have the same rights. Even while he was in jail, his fellow citizens saw him as the leader of the anti-apartheid movement.

World leaders put pressure on the South African government. They demanded Nelson's release. So, in 1990, Nelson was set free. Around the world people cheered. He gained political power for the nation's blacks in a peaceful way. In 1993, he won the Nobel Peace Prize. The next year he was elected president. In 1996, Nelson signed into law a new South African constitution. It guaranteed freedom of speech and all people's rights.

Check Your Understanding

1. Why was Nelson Mandela in jail?
   a. He threatened a police officer.
   b. He spray painted slogans on people's homes.
   c. He refused to do work.
   d. He spoke out against apartheid.

2. In what year did Nelson win the Nobel Peace Prize?
   a. 1981   c. 1993
   b. 1990   d. 1996

3. Nelson was kept in prison for more than
   a. 9 years.   c. 29 years.
   b. 27 years.   d. 32 years.

4. Why did world leaders pressure the South African government to release Nelson?
   a. They wanted South Africa to allow other countries to send mail into the nation.
   b. They believed all prisoners should be set free.
   c. They hoped Nelson Mandela would win the Nobel Peace Prize.
   d. They wanted apartheid to end.

/4

Warm-Up
26

Name _____

Mary Cassatt, Impressionist Artist

When Mary Cassatt was born in 1844, few women were educated. Even fewer women were artists. Yet while she was still a teen, Mary knew that she was meant to paint. She was willing to do whatever it took to follow her dream.

Mary was born in Pennsylvania. She and her family lived in Europe when she was young. They went to the great art galleries. Mary loved to look at the paintings. When she turned 15, she said she was going to art school. Her father said he'd rather see her dead than let her go to college! When she didn't back down, he let her go. But she found that American schools did not take female artists seriously. So she went to Paris, France, to study.

Mary worked night and day to improve her artwork. In 1868, an **art gallery** called the Paris Salon showed her paintings. It displayed more of them in 1872 and 1873. Her career was launched! Yet Mary broke away from the Paris Salon. She joined the impressionists. These people painted in a new style. They used obvious brushstrokes. They emphasized light and movement. Mary painted mothers and children in everyday poses.

Sadly, Mary went blind in 1915. She had to stop painting. She is remembered today as one of America's greatest painters.

Check Your Understanding

1. Mary Cassatt most liked to paint
   a. children.
   b. flowers.
   c. landscapes.
   d. famous people.

2. In what year did Mary have to stop painting?
   a. 1868
   b. 1872
   c. 1873
   d. 1915

3. An **art gallery** is a place where people
   a. learn how to paint.
   b. restore old paintings.
   c. purchase artwork.
   d. view sporting events.

4. Mary's father didn't want her to attend art school because back then
   a. art supplies were very expensive.
   b. very few women went to college.
   c. art schools would not accept female students.
   d. the fumes from paint caused blindness.

/4

Warm-Up 27

Name _____

Dr. Francisco Bravo

How do fresh fruits and vegetables get from the fields where they grow to the store? **Migrant** farm workers pick the crops by hand. They pack the food into boxes. These boxes go to your store.

Migrant farm workers move from place to place. They follow the crops as they ripen. Whole families, including children, work in the fields. They earn so little money that they struggle to make ends meet. Sometimes they get very sick. Yet they have no money for medical help. Francisco Bravo was a migrant worker. He decided to make a difference.

Bravo was born in California in 1910. His family came from Mexico. The whole family worked as migrants. After high

school, Bravo went to college. To pay for it, he worked two jobs during the school year. He did migrant work in the summer. Then he won a scholarship to medical school.

Bravo never forgot about the other migrant workers. He knew that most could not pay for health care. So after he earned his medical degree, he opened a medical clinic in 1938. The Bravo Clinic in Los Angeles gave free care to any needy Mexican American. Later, he gave migrant students scholarships to become doctors.

Check Your Understanding

1. A **migrant** is a person who
    a. moves from place to place.
    b. plans to become a doctor.
    c. never leaves home.
    d. owns a farm.

2. Which event occurred first?
    a. Bravo went to medical school.
    b. Bravo worked as a migrant worker.
    c. Bravo helped students to go to college.
    d. Bravo started at his own medical clinic.

3. Most migrant farm workers
    a. become doctors.
    b. have an easy life.
    c. have good medical care.
    d. don't get a good education.

4. Which statement is false?
    a. Bravo's family came to America from Mexico.
    b. Bravo spent years working as a migrant.
    c. The Bravo Clinic was built to help African Americans.
    d. Bravo had a scholarship to help him pay for medical school.

/4

Name _____

Hallie Daggett, First Female Lookout

President Theodore Roosevelt wanted to preserve natural places. He wanted everyone to have a chance to enjoy nature. So, in 1905, he formed the United States Forest Service. (It is now part of the National Park Service.)

In 1910, there were forest fires. Thousands of acres burned. The Service built fire watch towers. They put a tiny building on top of the tallest peak in an area. One person lived in this lonely spot and kept a constant watch for fires. The lookout let the fire departments know if there was trouble. By reacting quickly, the firemen kept the fires at bay.

In 1913, Hallie M. Daggett was the first female lookout hired. She worked in Klamath National Forest. It is in northern California. She made the difficult three-hour climb to Eddy's Gulch Lookout Station. It was atop Klamath Peak. She lived there from June through November for 15 years. She never left the tower during those months. Her sister climbed the mountain each week. She brought her supplies and mail.

In her first year, Hallie sighted 40 fires. She reported them so fast that just five acres burned! Her boss, Ranger M. H. McCarthy, was thrilled. He wrote, "Had one less faithful been the lookout, it might have been 5,000 acres. The first woman guardian is one big success."

Today, satellites watch for wildfires.

Check Your Understanding

1. The job of a lookout was to
   a. report fires.
   b. watch over wildlife.
   c. fight fires.
   d. photograph wildlife.

2. Today, the U.S. Forest Service is
   a. hundreds of years old.
   b. no longer concerned with forest fires.
   c. hiring lookouts for the fire watch towers.
   d. a part of the National Park Service.

3. Hallie Daggett lived in a fire watch tower
   a. year round from 1913 until 1928.
   b. on top of Klamath Peak.
   c. and never spotted a fire.
   d. for one summer.

4. During her time as a lookout, Hallie probably felt
   a. terrified.
   b. annoyed.
   c. lonely.
   d. unimportant.

/4

Warm-Up

29 — **Jim Thorpe, Extraordinary Athlete**

Name _____

Many people view Jim Thorpe as one of the greatest athletes ever. He excelled in track-and-field events. He was a pro football and baseball player. Jim was a Native American. He was born in Oklahoma in 1887. While he was in high school, his amazing athletic skills were noticed.

Sweden hosted the 1912 Olympic Games. Jim went to the Games. He made headlines around the world. Jim came in first in the 200-meter dash and the 1,500-meter run. He was also the first athlete to win both the pentathlon and decathlon!

The pentathlon has five events. They are horseback riding, fencing (sword play with a foil instead of a sword), pistol shooting, swimming, and cross-country running. The decathlon has ten events. The athlete must run three races and jump hurdles. He must throw the discus, javelin, and shot put. He must also do the high jump, long jump, and pole vault. No wonder the king of Sweden called Jim "the greatest athlete in the world." It is very rare for one athlete to do so well in so many sports.

Jim went on to play pro baseball for three major league teams. He played pro football for seven teams. In 1951, he was one of the first players inducted into the National Football Hall of Fame.

Check Your Understanding

1. Swimming is one of the events in the
   a. Hall of Fame.
   b. Winter Olympic Games.
   c. pentathlon.
   d. decathlon.

2. Jim Thorpe played as a professional athlete in
   a. hockey.
   b. baseball.
   c. soccer.
   d. basketball.

3. Why did the Swedish king call Jim "the greatest athlete in the world"?
   a. Jim excelled in a wide variety of sports.
   b. Jim showed good sportsmanship whenever he lost.
   c. In high school, people recognized that Jim had athletic talent.
   d. Jim was a Native American.

4. In which event did Thorpe win an Olympic gold medal?
   a. fencing
   b. javelin
   c. 800-meter run
   d. decathlon

/4

Name _____

Norman Rockwell, the People's Artist

Norman Rockwell was born in 1894. When he was nine, his family moved. To get along with the kids at his new school, he drew pictures for them. He was talented. By the age of 18, he was the art director for *Boys' Life* magazine.

Norman submitted five paintings to the editor of the *Saturday Evening Post*. These pictures became the front covers for the magazine. It was the start of his main career. He created 318 covers for the *Post* during the next 47 years. His paintings gave a glimpse into the daily lives of ordinary Americans. They are some of the most beloved pictures in America. You may have seen his Thanksgiving one. In it, a gray-haired grandma places a turkey on a table. Grandpa stands beside her. Nine people sit at the table.

Norman used a detailed process to make each of his paintings. First, he sketched the scene. Next, he made individual drawings of each item in the scene. Then, he made charcoal drawings of the entire scene. Last, he made a color sketch of the whole scene. Only then, did he pick up his paintbrush and do the actual painting!

Fire destroyed his studio in 1943. Many of his paintings were lost. He continued to paint until he died in 1978.

Check Your Understanding

1. How many covers did Norman do for the *Saturday Evening Post*?
   a. 47
   b. 189
   c. 318
   d. 5

2. In creating a painting, which step did Norman do second?
   a. He sketched the whole scene.
   b. He made charcoal line drawings of the scene.
   c. He made a color sketch of the scene.
   d. He did drawings of each individual item.

3. When he was 18, Norman worked as a(n)
   a. magazine editor.
   b. art director.
   c. art teacher.
   d. *Boys' Life* writer.

4. Why were Norman's paintings so popular?
   a. He captured everyday scenes to which people could relate.
   b. He painted famous people that everyone liked.
   c. He made large paintings.
   d. He did charcoal line drawings before the actual painting.

/4

Answer Key

168

Answer Key

Interesting Places and Events

Page 9 Australia
1. b
2. d
3. a
4. c

Page 10 Hostage Rescue in Peru
1. d
2. c
3. b
4. a

Page 11 Big Blast in Siberia
1. b
2. d
3. a
4. c

Page 12 The Discovery of New Zealand
1. c
2. b
3. d
4. c

Page 13 Maine, the Blueberry State
1. b
2. a
3. d
4. b

Page 14 The Death of the Aral Sea
1. c
2. d
3. c
4. a

Page 15 The Year Without a Summer
1. c
2. b
3. c
4. a

Page 16 The Faces of Mount Rushmore
1. b
2. c
3. d
4. b

Page 17 The Smithsonian Institute
1. a
2. a
3. c
4. b

Page 18 The Rocky Mountains
1. d
2. d
3. a
4. c

Page 19 Rhode Island, the Smallest State
1. a
2. b
3. d
4. c

Page 20 The Amazon Rain Forest
1. c
2. b
3. d
4. a

Page 21 The Galapagos Islands
1. a
2. c
3. d
4. b

Page 22 The California Gold Rush
1. c
2. b
3. d
4. d

Page 23 The Earthquakes of 2010
1. b
2. c
3. a
4. b

Page 24 The Cruelest Month in American Mining
1. c
2. b
3. d
4. a

Page 25 The Deadly Cloud from Lake Nyos
1. c
2. b
3. a
4. d

Page 26 Signs of Global Warming
1. b
2. a
3. b
4. c

Page 27 Mount Kilimanjaro
1. b
2. c
3. a
4. a

Page 28 Antarctica
1. a
2. b
3. c
4. d

Page 29 Bermuda
1. b
2. d
3. b
4. c

Page 30 Mount Vernon
1. c
2. c
3. d
4. b

Page 31 Key West, Florida
1. d
2. b
3. c
4. a

Page 32 Without Warning
1. c
2. b
3. b
4. d

Page 33 The Great Yellowstone Fire of 1988
1. b
2. a
3. c
4. d

Page 34 The Bahamas
1. d
2. b
3. a
4. c

Page 35 Egypt: One Nation, Two Continents
1. a
2. d
3. c
4. b

Page 36 Arizona's Natural Wonders
1. d
2. c
3. b
4. a

Page 37 "Houston, We've Had a Problem"
1. c
2. d
3. b
4. a

Page 38 John Brown's Raid on Harper's Ferry
1. b
2. c
3. b
4. b

Scientifically Speaking

Page 41 Giant Panda Problems
1. c
2. d
3. d
4. a

Answer Key (cont.)

Page 42 The Great Alaskan Earthquake
1. b
2. a
3. d
4. c

Page 43 P-U! It's a Skunk!
1. b
2. c
3. d
4. a

Page 44 Insects
1. d
2. b
3. c
4. a

Page 45 Fearsome Fossil
1. c
2. a
3. b
4. b

Page 46 Surprises in the Sea
1. d
2. c
3. a
4. b

Page 47 Robots at Work
1. a
2. a
3. b
4. c

Page 48 Wildfires
1. c
2. d
3. a
4. d

Page 49 Disrupting Ecosystems
1. c
2. a
3. a
4. d

Page 50 Peppered Moths
1. b
2. d
3. c
4. a

Page 51 Neat Facts About Your Circulatory System
1. c
2. b
3. c
4. a

Page 52 Wind Energy
1. b
2. c
3. d
4. a

Page 53 Killer Bees Calming Down
1. b
2. a
3. d
4. a

Page 54 Trees Tell About Climates of the Past
1. c
2. d
3. b
4. a

Page 55 Snapping Turtles
1. b
2. d
3. a
4. b

Page 56 Eyelids
1. a
2. a
3. d
4. b

Page 57 Solar Storms
1. b
2. d
3. a
4. a

Page 58 Breeding Bunnies
1. d
2. a
3. c
4. b

Page 59 Glaciers
1. d
2. c
3. a
4. a

Page 60 Geothermal Energy
1. b
2. d
3. a
4. c

Page 61 Turning Soda Bottles into Blankets
1. a
2. b
3. d
4. d

Page 62 Using Two Legs Instead of Four
1. c
2. d
3. b
4. a

Page 63 Exciting News About Stem Cells
1. c
2. b
3. d
4. c

Page 64 Animal Instincts
1. c
2. a
3. b
4. c

Page 65 Volcanic Eruptions
1. d
2. a
3. d
4. c

Page 66 Live a Green Lifestyle
1. d
2. a
3. c
4. d

Page 67 Understanding Hemispheres
1. c
2. c
3. d
4. a

Page 68 Using Waste to Make Electricity
1. d
2. b
3. a
4. c

Page 69 Solar Energy
1. b
2. b
3. c
4. d

Page 70 Adapting to Global Warming
1. b
2. d
3. b
4. c

From the Past

Page 73 Where Did Everyone Go?
1. c
2. a
3. b
4. d

Page 74 Did George Washington Fight at Gettysburg?
1. a
2. b
3. d
4. c

Answer Key (cont.)

Page 75 **Iceboxes: The First Refrigerators**
1. c
2. a
3. b
4. d

Page 76 **The U.S. Civil War**
1. b
2. c
3. a
4. d

Page 77 **The Montgomery Bus Boycott**
1. a
2. a
3. d
4. c

Page 78 **How U.S. Libraries Began**
1. c
2. a
3. d
4. b

Page 79 **The Orphan Trains**
1. d
2. b
3. c
4. d

Page 80 **Braille for the Blind**
1. d
2. a
3. d
4. c

Page 81 **The Invention of the Microwave Oven**
1. b
2. a
3. d
4. c

Page 82 **The World's First Robot and His Dog**
1. d
2. b
3. a
4. d

Page 83 **How Plumbing Changed America**
1. a
2. c
3. d
4. b

Page 84 **Highway History**
1. d
2. c
3. a
4. a

Page 85 **The Buried Village of Ozette**
1. d
2. c
3. c
4. a

Page 86 **World War II Spies**
1. c
2. b
3. d
4. a

Page 87 **Inventions that Use Electricity**
1. c
2. c
3. b
4. d

Page 88 **Skiing**
1. b
2. c
3. a
4. c

Page 89 **The Great Liberty Bell Adventure**
1. a
2. d
3. a
4. b

Page 90 **Massachusetts Promotes Education**
1. d
2. c
3. b
4. d

Page 91 **Decoding Hieroglyphs**
1. d
2. a
3. c
4. a

page 92 **Canned Foods**
1. c
2. d
3. c
4. b

Page 93 **America's First Master Spy**
1. a
2. b
3. a
4. a

Page 94 **Amazing Ancient Structures**
1. c
2. d
3. a
4. c

Page 95 **The Ice Ages**
1. d
2. b
3. a
4. d

Page 96 **U.S. Anti-Slavery Laws**
1. a
2. b
3. c
4. d

Page 97 **U.S. Presidents from Ohio**
1. c
2. a
3. d
4. b

Page 98 **Flight Disappearances**
1. d
2. c
3. a
4. b

Page 99 **Moving the U.S. Mail, 1753 to 1863**
1. d
2. b
3. c
4. a

Page 100 **Moving the U.S. Mail, 1902 to Now**
1. c
2. d
3. c
4. b

Page 101 **Native American Unsolved Mysteries**
1. c
2. d
3. b
4. a

Page 102 **Washington Irving, Author and Ghost**
1. c
2. b
3. d
4. c

Did You Know?

Page 105 **Sea Horses**
1. b
2. c
3. a
4. d

Page 106 **The Popular Product That Almost Wasn't**
1. a
2. d
3. d
4. c

Answer Key (cont.)

Page 107 Not So Identical
1. a
2. b
3. d
4. a

Page 108 What You Didn't Know About George Washington
1. c
2. b
3. c
4. a

Page 109 In-Line Skates
1. d
2. b
3. c
4. d

Page 110 Mazes
1. c
2. d
3. c
4. c

Page 111 Guide Dogs
1. b
2. c
3. b
4. d

Page 112 Frozen Animals Stay Alive
1. c
2. a
3. b
4. d

Page 113 Binti Jua and Jambo to the Rescue
1. d
2. c
3. b
4. a

Page 114 The U.S. Supreme Court
1. c
2. d
3. c
4. a

Page 115 The World's Most Dangerous Animals
1. b
2. c
3. d
4. a

Page 116 Rice Feeds the World
1. c
2. a
3. a
4. d

Page 117 Bamboo
1. d
2. a
3. b
4. c

Page 118 Yawning *is* Contagious
1. a
2. b
3. a
4. d

Page 119 The Story of Jeep
1. d
2. b
3. a
4. d

Page 120 World's Largest Ice Sculptures: Icebergs
1. c
2. b
3. d
4. a

Page 121 Storms that Caused Discoveries
1. d
2. b
3. c
4. a

Page 122 The Sweet Story of Jelly Beans
1. b
2. a
3. c
4. d

Page 123 Pelorus Jack
1. a
2. b
3. c
4. a

Page 124 The Gulf Stream
1. b
2. c
3. d
4. b

Page 125 Snowboarding
1. a
2. b
3. c
4. d

Page 126 Dandelions: Weed, Flowers, or Food?
1. a
2. b
3. a
4. c

Page 127 The Weight, the Wind, and the Wobbling
1. a
2. c
3. d
4. b

Page 128 Heinz 57 Varieties
1. b
2. d
3. a
4. c

Page 129 Wacky Waterspouts
1. c
2. d
3. a
4. d

Page 130 Unique Languages
1. c
2. b
3. a
4. d

Page 131 Naming the States
1. a
2. b
3. a
4. d

Page 132 Mysteries in Peru
1. c
2. d
3. b
4. a

Page 133 The Story of Pizza
1. d
2. a
3. b
4. c

Page 134 The Indy 500
1. d
2. b
3. c
4. d

Fascinating People

Page 137 Dr. Antonia Novella, Former Surgeon General
1. c
2. b
3. a
4. a

Page 138 Dr. Elizabeth Blackwell, First U.S. Female Doctor
1. a
2. a
3. b
4. d

Page 139 Sojourner Truth, Civil Rights Leader
1. b
2. d
3. c
4. b

Page 140 The Angel of Marye's Heights
1. d
2. a
3. d
4. c

Answer Key (cont.)

Page 141 Barbara Jordan, Former U.S. Congresswoman
1. d
2. c
3. b
4. a

Page 142 Garrett Morgan, Inventor
1. a
2. d
3. c
4. b

Page 143 Mary McLeod Bethune, Educator
1. a
2. b
3. c
4. d

Page 144 Will Cross, Adventurer
1. b
2. d
3. a
4. c

Page 145 Louis Pasteur, the Milk Man
1. d
2. c
3. b
4. a

Page 146 The First Woman in Space
1. c
2. b
3. c
4. d

Page 147 I. M. Pei, Architect
1. d
2. c
3. b
4. a

Page 148 Delvin Miller, Harness Racing Master
1. c
2. b
3. a
4. d

Page 149 Asa Philip Randolph, Civil Rights Leader
1. c
2. a
3. d
4. b

Page 150 Jason McElwain, Basketball Star
1. b
2. a
3. b
4. d

Page 151 Loreta Velasquez, Civil War Soldier
1. b
2. c
3. a
4. b

Page 152 Clara Hale's House
1. c
2. b
3. a
4. c

Page 153 Wilma Mankiller, Former Cherokee Chief
1. d
2. a
3. c
4. d

Page 154 Dr. Susan La Flesche Picotte
1. d
2. a
3. b
4. c

Page 155 William Wilberforce, British Abolitionist
1. b
2. d
3. c
4. c

Page 156 Bethany Hamilton, Fearless Surfer
1. c
2. a
3. b
4. a

Page 157 Mother Jones, Labor Activitist
1. d
2. a
3. b
4. c

Page 158 The Wizard of Menlo Park
1. c
2. b
3. d
4. a

Page 159 Margaret Bourke-White, Photographer
1. b
2. c
3. d
4. c

Page 160 Terry Fox's Marathon of Hope
1. b
2. d
3. a
4. c

Page 161 Nelson Mandela, South African Leader
1. d
2. c
3. b
4. d

Page 162 Mary Cassatt, Impressionist Artist
1. a
2. d
3. c
4. b

Page 163 Dr. Francisco Bravo
1. a
2. b
3. d
4. c

Page 164 Hallie Daggett, First Female Lookout
1. a
2. d
3. b
4. c

Page 165 Jim Thorpe, Extraordinary Athlete
1. c
2. b
3. a
4. d

Page 166 Norman Rockwell, the People's Artist
1. c
2. d
3. b
4. a

Self-Monitoring Reading Strategies

Use these steps with your students so they can monitor their own reading comprehension. Be sure to go over each step with the class. Distribute a copy to each student or enlarge to make a class poster.

✐ Step 1: Do I Understand?

Read a paragraph. Then ask, "Do I totally understand everything in this paragraph?" Use a pencil to mark a light **X** next to each paragraph that you comprehend and a light question mark next to each paragraph that contains anything you do not understand.

✐ Step 2: What Have I Just Read?

At the end of each paragraph, stop and summarize silently to yourself, in your own words, what you have read. You may look back at the text during this activity.

✐ Step 3: Does It Make Sense Now?

Finish reading the passage. Return to each paragraph that has a penciled question mark next to it and reread it. Does it make sense now? If so, great! If not, move on to step 4.

✐ Step 4: Why Am I Having This Trouble?

Pinpoint the problem. Is the difficulty to do with unfamiliar words or concepts? Is the sentence structure too complex? Is it because you know little background information about the topic? It's important that you identify the specific stumbling block(s) before you move on to step 5.

✐ Step 5: Where Can I Get Help?

Try a variety of aids to help you understand the text: Internet, glossary, appendix, dictionary, thesaurus, encyclopedia, chapter summary, etc. Depending on what you are reading, use the resource(s) that will help you the most. If confusion remains after going through these five steps, ask a classmate or teacher for assistance.

As students become more comfortable with this strategy, you may want to make a rule that the students cannot ask for help from you unless they can do the following:

• identify the exact source of their confusion

• describe the steps they've already taken on their own to resolve the problem

Leveling Chart

Page #	Flesch-Kincaid Grade Level	Page #	Flesch-Kincaid Grade Level	Page #	Flesch-Kincaid Grade Level
Interesting Places and Events		**Scientifically Speaking** (cont.)		**Did You Know?** (cont.)	
9	5.2*	62	4.6	116	4.4
10	4.3	63	4.8	117	4.3
11	4.4	64	4.7	118	4.8
12	4.2	65	5.4*	119	5.3*
13	4.6	66	4.9	120	4.9
14	4.4	67	6.3*	121	4.5
15	4.4	68	5.4*	122	4.7
16	4.5	69	4.8	123	4.8
17	5.3*	70	5.0	124	4.7
18	4.6	**From the Past**		125	4.6
19	4.8	73	4.0	126	4.7
20	5.2*	74	4.8	127	5.3*
21	4.7	75	4.7	128	4.7
22	4.6	76	4.3	129	4.7
23	4.8	77	4.5	130	5.1*
24	5.1*	78	4.6	131	4.9
25	5.0	79	4.3	132	5.3*
26	4.6	80	4.5	133	7.0*
27	4.8	81	4.7	134	6.2*
28	4.8	82	4.3	**Fascinating People**	
29	5.2*	83	4.7	137	4.8
30	4.8	84	5.3*	138	4.0
31	4.8	85	4.6	139	4.1
32	4.8	86	4.6	140	4.1
33	4.8	87	5.2*	141	5.9*
34	5.0	88	4.6	142	5.0
35	4.8	89	4.7	143	4.5
36	4.9	90	6.1*	144	4.6
37	4.8	91	4.5	145	4.0
38	5.0	92	4.8	146	5.5*
Scientifically Speaking		93	4.7	147	5.4*
41	4.2	94	4.8	148	5.2*
42	4.1	95	5.2*	149	5.1*
43	4.3	96	4.9	150	4.5
44	4.6	97	5.1*	151	4.6
45	4.5	98	4.9	152	4.6
46	4.6	99	5.1*	153	4.7
47	4.2	100	4.9	154	4.7
48	4.9	101	4.9	155	4.9
49	4.4	102	4.9	156	4.7
50	4.7	**Did You Know?**		157	5.0
51	4.4	105	4.1	158	5.9*
52	4.6	106	4.0	159	4.7
53	4.2	107	4.0	160	4.8
54	4.6	108	4.4	161	5.0
55	4.7	109	4.1	162	4.9
56	4.6	110	4.6	163	5.0
57	4.7	111	4.3	164	5.0
58	4.5	112	4.3	165	5.2*
59	5.2*	113	4.3	166	4.8
60	4.8	114	4.3		
61	4.8	115	4.3		

Tracking Sheet

Interesting Places and Events		Scientifically Speaking		From the Past		Did You Know?		Fascinating People	
Page 9		Page 41		Page 73		Page 105		Page 137	
Page 10		Page 42		Page 74		Page 106		Page 138	
Page 11		Page 43		Page 75		Page 107		Page 139	
Page 12		Page 44		Page 76		Page 108		Page 140	
Page 13		Page 45		Page 77		Page 109		Page 141	
Page 14		Page 46		Page 78		Page 110		Page 142	
Page 15		Page 47		Page 79		Page 111		Page 143	
Page 16		Page 48		Page 80		Page 112		Page 144	
Page 17		Page 49		Page 81		Page 113		Page 145	
Page 18		Page 50		Page 82		Page 114		Page 146	
Page 19		Page 51		Page 83		Page 115		Page 147	
Page 20		Page 52		Page 84		Page 116		Page 148	
Page 21		Page 53		Page 85		Page 117		Page 149	
Page 22		Page 54		Page 86		Page 118		Page 150	
Page 23		Page 55		Page 87		Page 119		Page 151	
Page 24		Page 56		Page 88		Page 120		Page 152	
Page 25		Page 57		Page 89		Page 121		Page 153	
Page 26		Page 58		Page 90		Page 122		Page 154	
Page 27		Page 59		Page 91		Page 123		Page 155	
Page 28		Page 60		Page 92		Page 124		Page 156	
Page 29		Page 61		Page 93		Page 125		Page 157	
Page 30		Page 62		Page 94		Page 126		Page 158	
Page 31		Page 63		Page 95		Page 127		Page 159	
Page 32		Page 64		Page 96		Page 128		Page 160	
Page 33		Page 65		Page 97		Page 129		Page 161	
Page 34		Page 66		Page 98		Page 130		Page 162	
Page 35		Page 67		Page 99		Page 131		Page 163	
Page 36		Page 68		Page 100		Page 132		Page 164	
Page 37		Page 69		Page 101		Page 133		Page 165	
Page 38		Page 70		Page 102		Page 134		Page 166	